A PERSONAL RECORD

A PERSONAL RECORD

BY
JOSEPH CONRAD

GARDEN CITY   NEW YORK
DOUBLEDAY, PAGE & COMPANY
1924

AUTHOR'S NOTE

THE re-issue of this book in a new form does not strictly speaking require another Preface. But since this is distinctly a place for personal remarks I take the opportunity to refer in this Author's Note to two points arising from certain statements about myself I have noticed of late in the press.

One of them bears upon the question of language. I have always felt myself looked upon somewhat in the light of a phenomenon, a position which outside the circus world cannot be regarded as desirable. It needs a special temperament for one to derive much gratification from the fact of being able to do freakish things intentionally, and, as it were, from mere vanity.

The fact of my not writing in my native language has been of course commented upon frequently in reviews and notices of my various works and in the more extended critical articles. I suppose that was unavoidable; and indeed these comments were of the most flattering kind to one's vanity. But in that matter I have no vanity that could be flattered. I could not have it. The first object of this note is to disclaim any merit there might have been in an act of deliberate volition.

The impression of my having exercised a choice between the two languages, French and English, both foreign to me, has got abroad somehow. That impression is erroneous. It originated, I believe, in an article written by Sir Hugh Clifford and published in the year 98, I think, of the last century. Some time before,

Sir Hugh Clifford came to see me. He is, if not the first, then one of the first two friends I made for myself by my work, the other being Mr. Cunninghame Graham, who, characteristically enough, had been captivated by my story, *An Outpost of Progress*. These friendships which have endured to this day I count amongst my precious possessions.

Mr. Hugh Clifford (he was not decorated then) had just published his first volume of Malay sketches. I was naturally delighted to see him and infinitely gratified by the kind things he found to say about my first books and some of my early short stories, the action of which is placed in the Malay Archipelago. I remember that after saying many things which ought to have made me blush to the roots of my hair with outraged modesty, he ended by telling me with the uncompromising yet kindly firmness of a man accustomed to speak unpalatable truths even to Oriental potentates (for their own good of course) that as a matter of fact I didn't know anything about Malays. I was perfectly aware of this. I have never pretended to any such knowledge, and I was moved—I wonder to this day at my impertinence —to retort: "Of course I don't know anything about Malays. If I knew only one hundredth part of what you and Frank Swettenham know of Malays I would make everybody sit up." He went on looking kindly (but firmly) at me and then we both burst out laughing. In the course of that most welcome visit twenty years ago, which I remember so well, we talked of many things; the characteristics of various languages was one of them, and it is on that day that my friend carried away with him the impression that I had exercised a deliberate choice between French and English. Later, when moved by his friendship (no empty word to him) to write a study in the *North American Review* on

Joseph Conrad, he conveyed that impression to the public.

This misapprehension, for it is nothing else, was no doubt my fault. I must have expressed myself badly in the course of a friendly and intimate talk when one doesn't watch one's phrases carefully. My recollection of what I meant to say is: that *had I been under the necessity* of making a choice between the two, and though I knew French fairly well and was familiar with it from infancy, I would have been afraid to attempt expression in a language so perfectly "crystallized." This, I believe, was the word I used. And then we passed to other matters. I had to tell him a little about myself; and what he told me of his work in the East, his own particular East of which I had but the mistiest, short glimpse, was of the most absorbing interest. The present Governor of Nigeria may not remember that conversation as well as I do, but I am sure that he will not mind this, what in diplomatic language is called "rectification" of a statement made to him by an obscure writer his generous sympathy had prompted him to seek out and make his friend.

The truth of the matter is that my faculty to write in English is as natural as any other aptitude with which I might have been born. I have a strange and overpowering feeling that it had always been an inherent part of myself. English was for me neither a matter of choice nor adoption. The merest idea of choice had never entered my head. And as to adoption— well, yes, there was adoption; but it was I who was adopted by the genius of the language, which directly I came out of the stammering stage made me its own so completely that its very idioms I truly believe had a direct action on my temperament and fashioned my still plastic character.

It was a very intimate action and for that very reason it is too mysterious to explain. The task would be as impossible as trying to explain love at first sight. There was something in this conjunction of exulting, almost physical recognition, the same sort of emotional surrender and the same pride of possession, all united in the wonder of a great discovery; but there was on it none of that shadow of dreadful doubt that falls on the very flame of our perishable passions. One knew very well that this was for ever.

A matter of discovery and not of inheritance, that very inferiority of the title makes the faculty still more precious, lays the possessor under a lifelong obligation to remain worthy of his great fortune. But it seems to me that all this sounds as if I were trying to explain —a task which I have just pronounced to be impossible. If in action we may admit with awe that the Impossible recedes before men's indomitable spirit, the Impossible in matters of analysis will always make a stand at some point or other. All I can claim after all those years of devoted practice, with the accumulated anguish of its doubts, imperfections and falterings in my heart, is the right to be believed when I say that if I had not written in English I would not have written at all.

The other remark which I wish to make here is also a rectification but of a less direct kind. It has nothing to do with the medium of expression. It bears on the matter of my authorship in another way. It is not for me to criticise my judges, the more so because I always felt that I was receiving more than justice at their hands. But it seems to me that their unfailingly interested sympathy has ascribed to racial and historical influences much, of what, I believe, appertains simply to the individual. Nothing is more foreign than what in the literary world is called Sclavonism, to the Polish temperament with its tradition of self-government, its chivalrous view of moral restraints and an exaggerated respect for individual rights: not to mention the important fact that the whole Polish mentality, Western in complexion, had received its training from Italy and France and, historically, had always remained, even in religious matters, in sympathy with the most liberal currents of European thought. An impartial view of humanity in all its degrees of splendour and misery together with a special regard for the rights of the unprivileged of this earth, not on any mystic ground but on the ground of simple fellowship and honourable reciprocity of services, was the dominant characteristic of the mental and moral atmosphere of the houses which sheltered my hazardous childhood:—matters of calm and deep conviction both lasting and consistent, and removed as far as possible from that humanitarianism that seems to be merely a matter of crazy nerves or a morbid conscience.

One of the most sympathetic of my critics tried to account for certain characteristics of my work by the fact of my being, in his own words, "the son of a Revolutionist." No epithet could be more inapplicable to a man with such a strong sense of responsibility in the region of ideas and action and so indifferent to the promptings of personal ambition as my father. Why the description "revolutionary" should have been applied all through Europe to the Polish risings of 1831 and 1863 I really cannot understand. These risings were purely revolts against foreign domination. The Russians themselves called them "rebellions," which, from their point of view, was the exact truth. Amongst the men concerned in the preliminaries of the 1863 movement my father was no more revolutionary than the others, in the sense of working for the subversion of any social or political scheme of existence. He was simply a patriot in the sense of a man who believing in the spirituality of a national existence could not bear to see that spirit enslaved.

Called out publicly in a kindly attempt to justify the work of the son, that figure of my past cannot be dismissed without a few more words. As a child of course I knew very little of my father's activities, for I was not quite twelve when he died. What I saw with my own eyes was the public funeral, the cleared streets, the hushed crowds; but I understood perfectly well that this was a manifestation of the national spirit seizing a worthy occasion. That bareheaded mass of work people, youths of the University, women at the windows, school-boys on the pavement, could have known nothing positive about him except the fame of his fidelity to the one guiding emotion in their hearts. I had nothing but that knowledge myself; and this great silent demonstration seemed to me the most natural tribute in the world—not to the man but to the Idea.

What had impressed me much more intimately was the burning of his manuscripts a fortnight or so before his death. It was done under his own superintendence. I happened to go into his room a little earlier than usual that evening, and remaining unnoticed stayed to watch the nursing-sister feeding the blaze in the fireplace. My father sat in a deep armchair propped up with pillows. This was the last time I saw him out of bed. His aspect was to me not so much that of a man desperately ill, as mortally weary—a vanquished man. That act of destruction affected me profoundly by its air of surrender. Not before death however. To a man of such strong faith death could not have been an enemy.

For many years I believed that every scrap of his

writings had been burnt, but in July of 1914 the Librarian of the University of Cracow calling on me during our short visit to Poland, mentioned the existence of a few manuscripts of my father and especially of a series of letters written before and during his exile to his most intimate friend who had sent them to the University for preservation. I went to the Library at once, but had only time then for a mere glance. I intended to come back next day and arrange for copies being made of the whole correspondence. But next day there was war. So perhaps I shall never know now what he wrote to his most intimate friend in the time of his domestic happiness, of his new paternity, of his strong hopes—and later, in the hours of disillusion, bereavement and gloom.

I had also imagined him to be completely forgotten forty-five years after his death. But this was not the case. Some young men of letters had discovered him, mostly as a remarkable translator of Shakespeare, Victor Hugo and Alfred de Vigny, to whose drama *Chatterton*, translated by himself, he had written an eloquent preface defending the poet's deep humanity and his ideal of noble stoicism. The political side of his life was being recalled too; for some men of his time, his co-workers in the task of keeping the national spirit firm in the hope of an independent future, had been in their old age publishing their memoirs, where the part he played was for the first time publicly disclosed to the world. I learned then of things in his life I never knew before, things which outside the group of the initiated could have been known to no living being except my mother. It was thus that from a volume of posthumous memoirs dealing with those bitter years I learned the fact that the first inception of the secret National Committee intended primarily to organize moral resistance

to the augmented pressure of Russianism arose on my
father's initiative, and that its first meetings were held
in our Warsaw house, of which all I remember distinctly
is one room, white and crimson, probably the drawing-
room. In one of its walls there was the loftiest of all
archways. Where it led to remains a mystery; but to
this day I cannot get rid of the belief that all this was of
enormous proportions, and that the people appearing
and disappearing in that immense space were beyond
the usual stature of mankind as I got to know it in later
life. Amongst them I remember my mother, a more
familiar figure than the others, dressed in the black of
the national mourning worn in defiance of ferocious
police regulations. I have also preserved from that
particular time the awe of her mysterious gravity which,
indeed, was by no means smileless. For I remember
her smiles, too. Perhaps for me she could always find a
smile. She was young then, certainly not yet thirty.
She died four years later in exile.

In the pages which follow I mention her visit to
her brother's house about a year before her death. I
also speak a little of my father as I remember him in
the years following what was for him the deadly blow of
her loss. And now, having been again evoked in answer to the words of a friendly critic, these Shades may
be allowed to return to their place of rest where their
forms in life linger yet, dim but poignant, and awaiting
the moment when their haunting reality, their last trace
on earth, shall pass for ever with me out of the world.

1919.   J. C.

A FAMILIAR PREFACE

As a general rule we do not want much encouragement to talk about ourselves; yet this little book is the result of a friendly suggestion, and even of a little friendly pressure. I defended myself with some spirit; but, with characteristic tenacity, the friendly voice insisted, "You know, you really must."

It was not an argument, but I submitted at once. If one must! . . .

You perceive the force of a word. He who wants to persuade should put his trust not in the right argument, but in the right word. The power of sound has always been greater than the power of sense. I don't say this by way of disparagement. It is better for mankind to be impressionable than reflective. Nothing humanely great—great, I mean, as affecting a whole mass of lives—has come from reflection. On the other hand, you cannot fail to see the power of mere words; such words as Glory, for instance, or Pity. I won't mention any more. They are not far to seek. Shouted with perseverance, with ardour, with conviction, these two by their sound alone have set whole nations in motion and upheaved the dry, hard ground on which rests our whole social fabric. There's "virtue" for you if you like! . . . Of course the accent must be attended to. The right accent. That's very important. The capacious lung, the thundering or the tender vocal chords. Don't talk to me of your Archimedes' lever. He was an absent-minded person with a mathematical imagination. Mathematics commands all my respect, but I have no use for engines. Give me the right word and the right accent and I will move the world.

What a dream for a writer! Because written words have their accent, too. Yes! Let me only find the right word! Surely it must be lying somewhere among the wreckage of all the plaints and all the exultations poured out aloud since the first day when hope, the undying, came down on earth. It may be there, close by, disregarded, invisible, quite at hand. But it's no good. I believe there are men who can lay hold of a needle in a pottle of hay at the first try. For myself, I have never had such luck.

And then there is that accent. Another difficulty. For who is going to tell whether the accent is right or wrong till the word is shouted, and fails to be heard, perhaps, and goes down-wind, leaving the world unmoved? Once upon a time there lived an emperor who was a sage and something of a literary man. He jotted down on ivory tablets thoughts, maxims, reflections which chance has preserved for the edification of posterity. Among other sayings—I am quoting from memory—I remember this solemn admonition: "Let all thy words have the accent of heroic truth." The accent of heroic truth! This is very fine, but I am thinking that it is an easy matter for an austere emperor to jot down grandiose advice. Most of the working truths on this earth are humble, not heroic; and there have been times in the history of mankind when the accents of heroic truth have moved it to nothing but derision.

Nobody will expect to find between the covers of this little book words of extraordinary potency or accents of irresistible heroism. However humiliating for my self-esteem, I must confess that the counsels of Marcus Aurelius are not for me. They are more fit for a moralist than for an artist. Truth of a modest sort I can promise you, and also sincerity. That complete, praiseworthy sincerity which, while it delivers one into the hands of one's enemies, is as likely as not to embroil one with one's friends.

"Embroil" is perhaps too strong an expression. I can't imagine among either my enemies or my friends a being so hard up for something to do as to quarrel with me. "To disappoint one's friends" would be nearer the mark. Most, almost all, friendships of the writing period of my life have come to me through my books; and I know that a novelist lives in his work. He stands there, the only reality in an invented world, among imaginary things, happenings, and people. Writing about them, he is only writing about himself. But the disclosure is not complete. He remains, to a certain extent, a figure behind the veil; a suspected rather than a seen presence—a movement and a voice behind the draperies of fiction. In these personal notes there is no such veil. And I cannot help thinking of a passage in the "Imitation of Christ" where the ascetic author, who knew life so profoundly, says that "there are persons esteemed on their reputation who by showing themselves destroy the opinion one had of them." This is the danger incurred by an author of fiction who sets out to talk about himself without disguise.

While these reminiscent pages were appearing serially I was remonstrated with for bad economy; as if such writing were a form of self-indulgence wasting the substance of future volumes. It seems that I am not sufficiently literary. Indeed, a man who never wrote a line for print till he was thirty-six cannot bring himself to look upon his existence and his experience, upon the sum of his thoughts, sensations, and emotions, upon his memories and his regrets, and the whole possession of his past, as only so much material for his hands. Once before, some three years ago, when I published "The Mirror of the Sea," a volume of impressions and memories, the same remarks were made to me. Practical remarks. But, truth to say, I have never understood the kind of thrift they recommend. I wanted to pay my tribute to the sea, its ships and its men, to whom I remain indebted for so much which has gone to make me what I am. That seemed to me the only shape in which I could offer it to their shades. There could not be a question in my mind of anything else. It is quite possible that I am a bad economist; but it is certain that I am incorrigible.

Having matured in the surroundings and under the special conditions of sea life, I have a special piety toward that form of my past; for its impressions were vivid, its appeal direct, its demands such as could be responded to with the natural elation of youth and strength equal to the call. There was nothing in them to perplex a young conscience. Having broken away from my origins under a storm of blame from every quarter which had the merest shadow of right to voice an opinion, removed by great distances from such natural affections as were still left to me, and even estranged, in a measure, from them by the totally unintelligible character of the life which had seduced me so mysteriously from my allegiance, I may safely say that through the blind force of circumstances the sea was to be all my world and the merchant service my only home for a long succession of years. No wonder, then, that in my two exclusively sea books—"The Nigger of the 'Narcissus,'" and "The Mirror of the Sea" (and in the few short sea stories like "Youth" and

"Typhoon")—I have tried with an almost filial regard to render the vibration of life in the great world of waters, in the hearts of the simple men who have for ages traversed its solitudes, and also that something sentient which seems to dwell in ships—the creatures of their hands and the objects of their care.

One's literary life must turn frequently for sustenance to memories and seek discourse with the shades, unless one has made up one's mind to write only in order to reprove mankind for what it is, or praise it for what it is not, or—generally—to teach it how to behave. Being neither quarrelsome, nor a flatterer, nor a sage, I have done none of these things, and I am prepared to put up serenely with the insignificance which attaches to persons who are not meddlesome in some way or other. But resignation is not indifference. I would not like to be left standing as a mere spectator on the bank of the great stream carrying onward so many lives. I would fain claim for myself the faculty of so much insight as can be expressed in a voice of sympathy and compassion.

It seems to me that in one, at least, authoritative quarter of criticism I am suspected of a certain unemotional, grim acceptance of facts—of what the French would call *sécheresse du cœur*. Fifteen years of unbroken silence before praise or blame testify sufficiently to my respect for criticism, that fine flower of personal expression in the garden of letters. But this is more of a personal matter, reaching the man behind the work, and therefore it may be alluded to in a volume which is a personal note in the margin of the public page. Not that I feel hurt in the least. The charge—if it amounted to a charge at all—was made in the most considerate terms; in a tone of regret.

My answer is that if it be true that every novel

contains an element of autobiography—and this can hardly be denied, since the creator can only express himself in his creation—then there are some of us to whom an open display of sentiment is repugnant. I would not unduly praise the virtue of restraint. It is often merely temperamental. But it is not always a sign of coldness. It may be pride. There can be nothing more humiliating than to see the shaft of one's emotion miss the mark of either laughter or tears. Nothing more humiliating! And this for the reason that should the mark be missed, should the open display of emotion fail to move, then it must perish unavoidably in disgust or contempt. No artist can be reproached for shrinking from a risk which only fools run to meet and only genius dares confront with impunity. In a task which mainly consists in laying one's soul more or less bare to the world, a regard for decency, even at the cost of success, is but the regard for one's own dignity which is inseparably united with the dignity of one's work.

And then—it is very difficult to be wholly joyous or wholly sad on this earth. The comic, when it is human, soon takes upon itself a face of pain; and some of our griefs (some only, not all, for it is the capacity for suffering which makes man august in the eyes of men) have their source in weaknesses which must be recognized with smiling compassion as the common inheritance of us all. Joy and sorrow in this world pass into each other, mingling their forms and their murmurs in the twilight of life as mysterious as an overshadowed ocean, while the dazzling brightness of supreme hopes lies far off, fascinating and still, on the distant edge of the horizon.

Yes! I, too, would like to hold the magic wand giving that command over laughter and tears which is declared to be the highest achievement of imaginative literature. Only, to be a great magician one must surrender oneself to occult and irresponsible powers, either outside or within one's breast. We have all heard of simple men selling their souls for love or power to some grotesque devil. The most ordinary intelligence can perceive without much reflection that anything of the sort is bound to be a fool's bargain. I don't lay claim to particular wisdom because of my dislike and distrust of such transactions. It may be my sea training acting upon a natural disposition to keep good hold on the one thing really mine, but the fact is that I have a positive horror of losing even for one moving moment that full possession of myself which is the first condition of good service. And I have carried my notion of good service from my earlier into my later existence. I, who have never sought in the written word anything else but a form of the Beautiful—I have carried over that article of creed from the decks of ships to the more circumscribed space of my desk, and by that act, I suppose, I have become permanently imperfect in the eyes of the ineffable company of pure esthetes.

As in political so in literary action a man wins friends for himself mostly by the passion of his prejudices and by the consistent narrowness of his outlook. But I have never been able to love what was not lovable or hate what was not hateful out of deference for some general principle. Whether there be any courage in making this admission I know not. After the middle turn of life's way we consider dangers and joys with a tranquil mind. So I proceed in peace to declare that I have always suspected in the effort to bring into play the extremities of emotions the debasing touch of insincerity. In order to move others deeply we must deliberately allow ourselves to be carried away beyond the bounds of our normal sensibility—innocently enough, perhaps, and of necessity, like an actor who raises his voice on the stage above the pitch of natural conversation—but still we have to do that. And surely this is no great sin. But the danger lies in the writer becoming the victim of his own exaggeration, losing the exact notion of sincerity, and in the end coming to despise truth itself as something too cold, too blunt for his purpose—as, in fact, not good enough for his insistent emotion. From laughter and tears the descent is easy to snivelling and giggles.

These may seem selfish considerations; but you can't, in sound morals, condemn a man for taking care of his own integrity. It is his clear duty. And least of all can you condemn an artist pursuing, however humbly and imperfectly, a creative aim. In that interior world where his thought and his emotions go seeking for the experience of imagined adventures, there are no policemen, no law, no pressure of circumstance or dread of opinion to keep him within bounds. Who then is going to say Nay to his temptations if not his conscience?

And besides—this, remember, is the place and the moment of perfectly open talk—I think that all ambitions are lawful except those which climb upward on the miseries or credulities of mankind. All intellectual and artistic ambitions are permissible, up to and even beyond the limit of prudent sanity. They can hurt no one. If they are mad, then so much the worse for the artist. Indeed, as virtue is said to be, such ambitions are their own reward. Is it such a very mad presumption to believe in the sovereign power of one's art, to try for other means, for other ways of affirming this belief in the deeper appeal of one's work? To try to go deeper is not to be insensible. An historian of hearts is not an historian of emotions, yet he penetrates further, restrained as he may be, since his aim is to reach the very fount of laughter and tears. The sight of human affairs deserves admiration and pity. They are worthy of respect, too. And he is not insensible who pays them the undemonstrative tribute of a sigh which is not a sob, and of a smile which is not a grin. Resignation, not mystic, not detached, but resignation open-eyed, conscious, and informed by love, is the only one of our feelings for which it is impossible to become a sham.

Not that I think resignation the last word of wisdom. I am too much the creature of my time for that. But I think that the proper wisdom is to will what the gods will without, perhaps, being certain what their will is— or even if they have a will of their own. And in this matter of life and art it is not the Why that matters so much to our happiness as the How. As the Frenchman said, "*Il y a toujours la manière.*" Very true. Yes. There is the manner. The manner in laughter, in tears, in irony, in indignations and enthusiasms, in judgments—and even in love. The manner in which, as in the features and character of a human face, the inner truth is foreshadowed for those who know how to look at their kind.

Those who read me know my conviction that the world, the temporal world, rests on a few very simple ideas; so simple that they must be as old as the hills. It rests notably, among others, on the idea of Fidelity. At a time when nothing which is not revolutionary in some way or other can expect to attract much attention I have not been revolutionary in my writings. The revolutionary spirit is mighty convenient in this, that it frees one from all scruples as regards ideas. Its hard, absolute optimism is repulsive to my mind by the menace of fanaticism and intolerance it contains. No doubt one should smile at these things; but, imperfect Esthete, I am no better Philosopher. All claim to special righteousness awakens in me that scorn and anger from which a philosophical mind should be free. . . .

I fear that trying to be conversational I have only managed to be unduly discursive. I have never been very well acquainted with the art of conversation—that art which, I understand, is supposed to be lost now. My young days, the days when one's habits and character are formed, have been rather familiar with long silences. Such voices as broke into them were anything but conversational. No. I haven't got the habit. Yet this discursiveness is not so irrelevant to the handful of pages which follow. They, too, have been charged with discursiveness, with disregard of chronological order (which is in itself a crime) with unconventionality of form (which is an impropriety). I was told severely that the public would view with displeasure the informal character of my recollections. "Alas!" I protested, mildly. "Could I begin with the sacramental words, 'I was born on such a date in such a place?' The remoteness of the locality would have robbed the statement of all interest. I haven't lived through wonderful adventures to be related *seriatim*. I haven't known distinguished men on whom I could pass fatuous remarks. I haven't been mixed up with great or scandalous affairs. This is but a bit of psychological document, and even so, I haven't written it with a view to put forward any conclusion of my own."

But my objector was not placated. These were good reasons for not writing at all—not a defence of what stood written already, he said.

I admit that almost anything, anything in the world, would serve as a good reason for not writing at all. But since I have written them, all I want to say in their defence is that these memories put down without any regard for established conventions have not been thrown off without system and purpose. They have their hope and their aim. The hope that from the reading of these pages there may emerge at last the vision of a personality; the man behind the books so fundamentally dissimilar as, for instance, "Almayer's Folly" and "The Secret Agent," and yet a coherent, justifiable personality both in its origin and in its action. This is the hope. The immediate aim, closely associated with the hope, is to give the record of personal memories by presenting faithfully the feelings and sensations connected with the writing of my first book and with my first contact with the sea.

In the purposely mingled resonance of this double strain a friend here and there will perhaps detect a subtle accord.

J. C.

A PERSONAL RECORD

A PERSONAL RECORD

I

Books may be written in all sorts of places. Verbal inspiration may enter the berth of a mariner on board a ship frozen fast in a river in the middle of a town; and since saints are supposed to look benignantly on humble believers, I indulge in the pleasant fancy that the shade of old Flaubert—who imagined himself to be (amongst other things) a descendant of Vikings—might have hovered with amused interest over the decks of a 2,000-ton steamer called the *Adowa*, on board of which, gripped by the inclement winter alongside a quay in Rouen, the tenth chapter of "Almayer's Folly" was begun. With interest, I say, for was not the kind Norman giant with enormous moustaches and a thundering voice the last of the Romantics? Was he not, in his unworldly, almost ascetic, devotion to his art a sort of literary, saint-like hermit?

"'*It has set at last,' said Nina to her mother, pointing to the hills behind which the sun had sunk.*" . . . These words of Almayer's romantic daughter I remember tracing on the grey paper of a pad which rested on the blanket of my bed-place. They referred to a sunset in Malayan Isles, and shaped themselves in my mind, in a hallucinated vision of forests and rivers and seas, far removed from a commercial and yet romantic town of the northern hemisphere. But at that moment the mood of visions and words was cut short by the third officer, a cheerful and casual youth, coming in with a bang of the door and the exclamation: "You've made it jolly warm in here."

It was warm. I had turned on the steam-heater after placing a tin under the leaky water-cock—for perhaps you do not know that water will leak where steam will not. I am not aware of what my young friend had been doing on deck all that morning, but the hands he rubbed together vigorously were very red and imparted to me a chilly feeling by their mere aspect. He has remained the only banjoist of my acquaintance, and being also a younger son of a retired colonel, the poem of Mr. Kipling, by a strange aberration of associated ideas, always seems to me to have been written with an exclusive view to his person. When he did not play the banjo he loved to sit and look at it. He proceeded to this sentimental inspection, and after meditating a while over the strings under my silent scrutiny, inquired airily:

"What are you always scribbling there, if it's fair to ask?"

It was a fair enough question, but I did not answer him, and simply turned the pad over with a movement of instinctive secrecy: I could not have told him he had put to flight the psychology of Nina Almayer, her opening speech of the tenth chapter and the words of Mrs. Almayer's wisdom which were to follow in the ominous oncoming of a tropical night. I could not have told him that Nina had said: "It has set at last." He would have been extremely surprised and perhaps have dropped his precious banjo. Neither could I have told him that the sun of my sea-going was setting too, even as I wrote the words expressing the impatience of passionate youth bent on its desire. I did not know this myself, and it is safe to say he would not have cared, though he was an excellent young fellow and treated me with more deference than, in our relative positions, I was strictly entitled to.

He lowered a tender gaze on his banjo and I went on looking through the port-hole. The round opening framed in its brass rim a fragment of the quays, with a row of casks ranged on the frozen ground and the tail-end of a great cart. A red-nosed carter in a blouse and a woollen nightcap leaned against the wheel. An idle, strolling custom-house guard, belted over his blue *capote*, had the air of being depressed by exposure to the weather and the monotony of official existence. The background of grimy houses found a place in the picture framed by my port-hole, across a wide stretch of paved quay, brown with frozen mud. The colouring was sombre, and the most conspicuous feature was a little *café* with curtained windows and a shabby front of white woodwork, corresponding with the squalor of these poorer quarters bordering the river. We had been shifted down there from another berth in the neighbourhood of the Opera House, where that same port-hole gave me a view of quite another sort of *café*— the best in the town, I believe, and the very one where the worthy Bovary and his wife, the romantic daughter of old Père Renault, had some refreshment after the memorable performance of an opera which was the tragic story of Lucia di Lammermoor in a setting of light music.

I could recall no more the hallucination of the Eastern Archipelago which I certainly hoped to see again. The story of "Almayer's Folly" got put away under the pillow for that day. I do not know that I had any occupation to keep me away from it; the truth of the matter is, that on board that ship we were leading just then a contemplative life. I will not say anything of my privileged position. I was there "just to oblige," as an actor of standing may take a small part in the benefit performance of a friend.

As far as my feelings were concerned, I did not wish to be in that steamer at that time and in those circumstances. And perhaps I was not even wanted there in the usual sense in which a ship "wants" an officer. It was the first and last instance in my sea life when I served ship-owners who have remained completely shadowy to my apprehension. I do not mean this for the well-known firm of London ship-brokers which had chartered the ship to the, I will not say short-lived, but ephemeral Franco-Canadian Transport Company. A death leaves something behind, but there was never anything tangible left from the F.C.T.C. It flourished no longer than roses live, and unlike the roses, it blossomed in the dead of winter, emitted a sort of faint perfume of adventure, and died before spring set in. But indubitably it was a company, it had even a house-flag, all white with the letters F.C.T.C. artfully tangled up in a complicated monogram. We flew it at our main-mast head, and now I have come to the conclusion that it was the only flag of its kind in existence. All the same, we on board, for many days, had the impression of being a unit of a large fleet with fortnightly departures for Montreal and Quebec as advertised in pamphlets and prospectuses which came aboard in a large package in Victoria Dock, London, just before we started for Rouen, France. And in the shadowy life of the F.C.T.C. lies the secret of that, my last employment in my calling, which in a remote sense interrupted the rhythmical development of Nina Almayer's story.

The then secretary of the London Shipmasters' Society, with its modest rooms in Fenchurch Street, was a man of indefatigable activity and the greatest devotion to his task. He is responsible for what was my last association with a ship. I call it that because it can hardly be called a sea-going experience. Dear Captain Froud—it is impossible not to pay him the tribute of affectionate familiarity at this distance of years—had very sound views as to the advancement of knowledge and status for the whole body of the officers of the mercantile marine. He organised for us courses of professional lectures, St. John Ambulance classes, corresponded industriously with public bodies and members of Parliament on subjects touching the interests of the service; and as to the oncoming of some inquiry or commission relating to matters of the sea and to the work of seamen, it was a perfect godsend to his need of exerting himself on our corporate behalf. Together with this high sense of his official duties he had in him a vein of personal kindness, a strong disposition to do what good he could to the individual members of that craft of which in his time he had been a very excellent master. And what greater kindness can one do to a seaman than to put him in the way of employment? Captain Froud did not see why the Shipmasters' Society, besides its general guardianship of our interests, should not be unofficially an employment agency of the very highest class.

"I am trying to persuade all our great ship-owning firms to come to us for their men. There is nothing of a trade-union spirit about our society and I really don't see why they should not," he said once to me. "I am always telling the captains, too, that all things being equal they ought to give preference to the members of the society. In my position I can generally find for them what they want amongst our members or our associate members."

In my wanderings about London from West to East

and back again (I was very idle then), the two little rooms in Fenchurch Street were a sort of resting-place where my spirit, hankering after the sea, could feel itself nearer to the ships, the men, and the life of its choice— nearer there than any other spot of the solid earth. This resting-place used to be, at about five o'clock in the afternoon, full of men and tobacco smoke, but Captain Froud had the smaller room to himself, and there he granted private interviews, whose principal motive was to render service. Thus, one murky November afternoon, he beckoned me in with a crooked finger and that peculiar glance above his spectacles which is perhaps my strongest physical recollection of the man.

"I have had in here a shipmaster this morning," he said, getting back to his desk and motioning me to a chair, "who is in want of an officer. It's for a steamship. You know, nothing pleases me more than to be asked, but unfortunately I do not quite see my way. . . ."

As the outer room was full of men, I cast a wondering glance at the closed door, but he shook his head.

"Oh, yes, I should be only too glad to get that berth for one of them. But the fact of the matter is, the captain of that ship wants an officer who can speak French fluently, and that's not so easy to find. I do not know anybody myself but you. It's a second officer's berth, and, of course, you would not care . . . would you now? I know that it isn't what you are looking for."

It was not. I had given myself up to the idleness of a haunted man who looks for nothing but words wherein to capture his visions. But I admit that outwardly I resembled sufficiently a man who could make a second officer for a steamer chartered by a French company.

I showed no sign of being haunted by the fate of Nina and by the murmurs of tropical forests; and even my intimate intercourse with Almayer (a person of weak character) had not put a visible mark upon my features. For many years he and the world of his story had been the companions of my imagination without, I hope, impairing my ability to deal with the realities of sea life. I had had the man and his surroundings with me ever since my return from the eastern waters, some four years before the day of which I speak.

It was in the front sitting-room of furnished apartments in a Pimlico square that they first began to live again with a vividness and poignancy quite foreign to our former real intercourse. I had been treating myself to a long stay on shore, and in the necessity of occupying my mornings, Almayer (that old acquaintance) came nobly to the rescue. Before long, as was only proper, his wife and daughter joined him round my table, and then the rest of that Pantai band came full of words and gestures. Unknown to my respectable landlady, it was my practice directly after my breakfast to hold animated receptions of Malays, Arabs and half-castes. They did not clamour aloud for my attention. They came with a silent and irresistible appeal—and the appeal, I affirm here, was not to my self-love or my vanity. It seems now to have had a moral character, for why should the memory of these beings, seen in their obscure sun-bathed existence, demand to express itself in the shape of a novel, except on the ground of that mysterious fellowship which unites in a community of hopes and fears all the dwellers on this earth?

I did not receive my visitors with boisterous rapture as the bearers of any gifts of profit or fame. There was no vision of a printed book before me as I sat writing at that table, situated in a decayed part of Belgravia. After all these years, each leaving its evidence of slowly blackened pages, I can honestly say that it is a sentiment akin to piety which prompted me to render in words assembled with conscientious care the memory of things far distant and of men who had lived.

But, coming back to Captain Froud and his fixed idea of never disappointing ship-owners or ship-captains, it was not likely that I should fail him in his ambition— to satisfy at a few hours' notice the unusual demand for a French-speaking officer. He explained to me that the ship was chartered by a French company intending to establish a regular monthly line of sailings from Rouen, for the transport of French emigrants to Canada. But, frankly, this sort of thing did not interest me very much. I said gravely that if it were really a matter of keeping up the reputation of the Shipmasters' Society, I would consider it. But the consideration was just for form's sake. The next day I interviewed the Captain, and I believe we were impressed favourably with each other. He explained that his chief mate was an excellent man in every respect, and that he could not think of dismissing him so as to give me the higher position; but that if I consented to come as second officer I would be given certain special advantages—and so on.

I told him that if I came at all the rank really did not matter.

"I am sure," he insisted, "you will get on first rate with Mr. Paramor."

I promised faithfully to stay for two trips at least, and it was in those circumstances that what was to be my last connection with a ship began. And after all there was not even one single trip. It may be that it was simply the fulfilment of a fate, of that written word on my forehead which apparently forbade me, through all my sea wanderings, ever to achieve the crossing of the Western Ocean—using the words in that special sense in which sailors speak of Western Ocean trade, of Western Ocean packets, of Western Ocean hard cases. The new life attended closely upon the old, and the nine chapters of "Almayer's Folly" went with me to the Victoria Dock, whence in a few days we started for Rouen. I won't go so far as saying that the engaging of a man fated never to cross the Western Ocean was the absolute cause of the Franco-Canadian Transport Company's failure to achieve even a single passage. It might have been that, of course; but the obvious, gross obstacle was clearly the want of money. Four hundred and sixty bunks for emigrants were put together in the 'tween decks by industrious carpenters while we lay in the Victoria Dock, but never an emigrant turned up in Rouen—of which, being a humane person, I confess I was glad. Some gentlemen from Paris—I think there were three of them, and one was said to be the Chairman—turned up indeed and went from end to end of the ship, knocking their silk hats cruelly against the deck-beams. I attended them personally, and I can vouch for it that the interest they took in things was intelligent enough, though, obviously they had never seen anything of the sort before. Their faces as they went ashore wore a cheerfully inconclusive expression. Notwithstanding that this inspecting ceremony was supposed to be a preliminary to immediate sailing, it was then, as they filed down our gangway, that I received the inward monition that no sailing within the meaning of our charter-party would ever take place.

It must be said that in less than three weeks a move took place. When we first arrived we had been taken up with much ceremony well towards the centre of the town, and, all the street corners being placarded with the tricolour posters announcing the birth of our company, the *petit bourgeois* with his wife and family made a Sunday holiday from the inspection of the ship. I was always in evidence in my best uniform to give information as though I had been a Cook's tourists' interpreter, while our quarter-masters reaped a harvest of small change from personally conducted parties. But when the move was made—that move which carried us some mile and a half down the stream to be tied up to an altogether muddier and shabbier quay—then indeed the desolation of solitude became our lot. It was a complete and soundless stagnation; for, as we had the ship ready for sea to the smallest detail, as the frost was hard and the days short, we were absolutely idle— idle to the point of blushing with shame when the thought struck us that all the time our salaries went on. Young Cole was aggrieved because, as he said, we could not enjoy any sort of fun in the evening after loafing like this all day: even the banjo lost its charm since there was nothing to prevent his strumming on it all the time between the meals. The good Paramor—he was really a most excellent fellow—became unhappy as far as was possible to his cheery nature, till one dreary day I suggested out of sheer mischief, that he should employ the dormant energies of the crew in hauling both cables up on deck and turning them end for end.

For a moment Mr. Paramor was radiant. "Excellent idea!" but directly his face fell. "Why . . . Yes! But we can't make that job last more than three days," he muttered discontentedly. I don't know how long he expected us to be stuck on the river-side outskirts of Rouen, but I know that the cables got hauled up and turned end for end according to my satanic suggestion, put down again, and their very existence utterly forgotten, I believe, before a French river pilot came on board to take our ship down, empty as she came, into the Havre roads. You may think that this state of forced idleness favoured some advance in the fortunes of Almayer and his daughter. Yet it was not so. As if it were some sort of evil spell, my banjoist cabin-mate's interruption, as related above, had arrested them short at the point of that fateful sunset for many weeks together. It was always thus with this book, begun in '89 and finished in '94—with that shortest of all the novels which it was to be my lot to write. Between its opening exclamation calling Almayer to his dinner in his wife's voice and Abdullah's (his enemy) mental reference to the God of Islam—"The Merciful, the Compassionate"—which closes the book, there were to come several long sea passages, a visit (to use the elevated phraseology suitable to the occasion) to the scenes (some of them) of my childhood and the realization of childhood's vain words, expressing a light-hearted and romantic whim.

It was in 1868, when nine years old or thereabouts, that while looking at a map of Africa of the time and putting my finger on the blank space then representing the unsolved mystery of that continent, I said to myself with absolute assurance and an amazing audacity which are no longer in my character now:

"When I grow up I shall go *there*."

And of course I thought no more about it till after a quarter of a century or so an opportunity offered to go there—as if the sin of childish audacity was to be visited on my mature head. Yes. I did go there: *there* being the region of Stanley Falls which in '68 was the blankest of blank spaces on the earth's figured surface. And the MS. of "Almayer's Folly," carried about me as if it were a talisman or a treasure, went *there* too.

That it ever came out of *there* seems a special dispensation of Providence; because a good many of my other properties, infinitely more valuable and useful to me, remained behind through unfortunate accidents of transportation.   I call to mind, for instance, a specially awkward turn of the Congo between Kinchassa and Leopoldsville—more particularly when one had to take it at night in a big canoe with only half the proper number of paddlers.   I failed in being the second white man on record drowned at that interesting spot through the upsetting of a canoe.   The first was a young Belgian officer, but the accident happened some months before my time, and he, too, I believe, was going home; not perhaps quite so ill as myself—but still he was going home.   I got round the turn more or less alive, though I was too sick to care whether I did or not, and, always with "Almayer's Folly" amongst my diminishing baggage, I arrived at that delectable capital Boma, where before the departure of the steamer which was to take me home I had the time to wish myself dead over and over again with perfect sincerity.   At that date there were in existence only seven chapters of "Almayer's Folly," but the chapter in my history which followed was that of a long, long illness and very dismal convalescence.   Geneva, or more precisely the hydropathic establishment of Champel, is rendered for ever famous by the termination of the eighth chapter in the history of Almayer's decline and fall.   The events of the ninth are inextricably mixed up with the details of the proper management of a waterside warehouse owned by a certain city firm whose name does not matter.   But that work, undertaken to accustom myself again to the activities of a healthy existence, soon came to an end.   The earth had nothing to hold me with for very long.   And then that memorable story, like a cask of choice Madeira, got carried for three years to and fro upon the sea. Whether this treatment improved its flavour or not, of course I would not like to say. As far as appearance is concerned, it certainly did nothing of the kind. The whole MS. acquired a faded look and an ancient, yellowish complexion. It became at last unreasonable to suppose that anything in the world would ever happen to Almayer and Nina. And yet something most unlikely to happen on the high seas was to wake them up from their state of suspended animation.

What is it that Novalis says? "It is certain my conviction gains infinitely the moment another soul will believe in it." And what is a novel if not a conviction of our fellow-men's existence strong enough to take upon itself a form of imagined life clearer than reality and whose accumulated verisimilitude of selected episodes puts to shame the pride of documentary history? Providence which saved my MS. from the Congo rapids brought it to the knowledge of a helpful soul far out on the open sea. It would be on my part the greatest ingratitude ever to forget the sallow, sunken face and the deep-set, dark eyes of the young Cambridge man (he was a "passenger for his health" on board the good ship *Torrens* outward bound to Australia) who was the first reader of "Almayer's Folly"—the very first reader I ever had. "Would it bore you very much reading a MS. in a handwriting like mine?" I asked him one evening on a sudden impulse at the end of a longish conversation whose subject was Gibbon's History. Jacques (that was his name) was sitting in my cabin one stormy dog-watch below, after bringing me a book to read from his own travelling store.

"Not at all," he answered with his courteous intonation and a faint smile. As I pulled a drawer open his suddenly aroused curiosity gave him a watchful expression. I wonder what he expected to see. A poem, maybe. All that's beyond guessing now. He was not a cold, but a calm man, still more subdued by disease—a man of few words and of an unassuming modesty in general intercourse, but with something uncommon in the whole of his person which set him apart from the undistinguished lot of our sixty passengers. His eyes had a thoughtful introspective look. In his attractive, reserved manner, and in a veiled, sympathetic voice, he asked:

"What is this?" "It is a sort of tale," I answered with an effort. "It is not even finished yet. Nevertheless, I would like to know what you think of it." He put the MS. in the breast-pocket of his jacket; I remember perfectly his thin brown fingers folding it lengthwise. "I will read it to-morrow," he remarked, seizing the door-handle, and then, watching the roll of the ship for a propitious moment, he opened the door and was gone. In the moment of his exit I heard the sustained booming of the wind, the swish of the water on the decks of the *Torrens*, and the subdued, as if distant, roar of the rising sea. I noted the growing disquiet in the great restlessness of the ocean, and responded professionally to it with the thought that at eight o'clock, in another half-hour or so at the furthest, the top-gallant sails would have to come off the ship.

Next day, but this time in the first dog-watch, Jacques entered my cabin. He had a thick, woollen muffler round his throat and the MS. was in his hand. He tendered it to me with a steady look but without a word. I took it in silence. He sat down on the couch and still said nothing. I opened and shut a drawer under my desk, on which a filled-up log-slate lay wide open in its wooden frame waiting to be copied neatly into the sort of book I was accustomed to write with care, the ship's log-book. I turned my back squarely on the desk. And even then Jacques never offered a word. "Well, what do you say?" I asked at last. "Is it worth finishing?" This question expressed exactly the whole of my thoughts.

"Distinctly," he answered in his sedate veiled voice, and then coughed a little.

"Were you interested?" I inquired further, almost in a whisper.

"Very much!"

In a pause I went on meeting instinctively the heavy rolling of the ship, and Jacques put his feet upon the couch. The curtain of my bed-place swung to and fro as it were a punkah, the bulkhead lamp circled in its gimbals, and now and then the cabin door rattled slightly in the gusts of wind. It was in latitude 40° south, and nearly in the longitude of Greenwich, as far as I can remember, that these quiet rites of Almayer's and Nina's resurrection were taking place. In the prolonged silence it occurred to me that there was a good deal of retrospective writing in the story as far as it went. Was it intelligible in its action, I asked myself, as if already the story-teller were being born into the body of a seaman. But I heard on deck the whistle of the officer of the watch and remained on the alert to catch the order that was to follow this call to attention. It reached me as a faint, fierce shout to "Square the yards." "Aha!" I thought to myself, "a westerly blow coming on." Then I turned to my very first reader, who, alas! was not to live long enough to know the end of the tale.

"Now let me ask you one more thing: Is the story quite clear to you as it stands?"

He raised his dark, gentle eyes to my face and seemed surprised.

"Yes! Perfectly."

This was all I was to hear from his lips concerning the merits of "Almayer's Folly." We never spoke together of the book again. A long period of bad weather set in and I had no thoughts left but for my duties, whilst poor Jacques caught a fatal cold and had to keep close in his cabin. When we arrived at Adelaide the first reader of my prose went at once up-country, and died rather suddenly in the end, either in Australia or it may be on the passage while going home through the Suez Canal. I am not sure which it was now, and I do not think I ever heard precisely; though I made inquiries about him from some of our return passengers who, wandering about to "see the country" during the ship's stay in port, had come upon him here and there. At last we sailed, homeward bound, and still not one line was added to the careless scrawl of the many pages which poor Jacques had had the patience to read with the very shadows of Eternity gathering already in the hollows of his kind, steadfast eyes.

The purpose instilled into me by his simple and final "Distinctly" remained dormant, yet alive to await its opportunity. I dare say I am compelled, unconsciously compelled, now to write volume after volume, as in past years I was compelled to go to sea, voyage after voyage. Leaves must follow upon each other as leagues used to follow in the days gone by, on and on to the appointed end, which, being Truth itself, is One—one for all men and for all occupations.

I do not know which of the two impulses has appeared more mysterious and more wonderful to me. Still, in writing, as in going to sea, I had to wait my opportunity. Let me confess here that I was never one of those wonderful fellows that would go afloat in a wash-tub for the sake of the fun, and if I may pride myself upon my consistency it was ever just the same with my writing. Some men, I have heard, write in railway carriages, and could do it, perhaps, sitting cross-legged on a clothes-line; but I must confess that my sybaritic disposition will not consent to write without something at least resembling a chair. Line by line, rather than page by page, was the growth of "Almayer's Folly."

And so it happened that I very nearly lost the MS., advanced now to the first words of the ninth chapter, in the Friedrichstrasse railway station (that's in Berlin, you know) on my way to Poland, or more precisely Ukraine. On an early, sleepy morning, changing trains in a hurry, I left my Gladstone bag in a refreshment-room. A worthy and intelligent *Kofferträger* rescued it. Yet in my anxiety I was not thinking of the MS. but of all the other things that were packed in the bag.

In Warsaw, where I spent two days, those wandering pages were never exposed to the light, except once, to candle-light, while the bag lay open on a chair. I was dressing hurriedly to dine at a sporting club. A friend of my childhood (he had been in the Diplomatic Service, but had turned to growing wheat on paternal acres, and we had not seen each other for over twenty years) was sitting on the hotel sofa waiting to carry me off there.

"You might tell me something of your life while you are dressing," he suggested kindly.

I do not think I told him much of my life-story either then or later. The talk of the select little party with which he made me dine was extremely animated and embraced most subjects under heaven, from big-game shooting in Africa to the last poem published in a very modernist review, edited by the very young and patronised by the highest society. But it never touched upon "Almayer's Folly," and next morning, in uninterrupted obscurity, this inseparable companion went on rolling with me in the south-east direction towards the Government of Kiev.

At that time there was an eight-hours' drive, if not more, from the railway station to the country house which was my destination.

"Dear boy" (these words were always written in English)—so ran the last letter from that house received in London—"Get yourself driven to the only inn in the place, dine as well as you can, and some time in the evening my own confidential servant, factotum and major-domo, a Mr. V. S. (I warn you he is of noble extraction), will present himself before you, reporting the arrival of the small sledge which will take you here on the next day. I send with him my heaviest fur, which I suppose, with such overcoats as you may have with you, will keep you from freezing on the road."

Sure enough, as I was dining, served by a Hebrew waiter, in an enormous barn-like bedroom with a freshly painted floor, the door opened and, in a travelling costume of long boots, big sheep-skin cap and a short coat girt with a leather belt, the Mr. V. S. (of noble extraction), a man of about thirty-five, appeared with an air of perplexity on his open and moustachioed countenance. I got up from the table and greeted him in Polish, with, I hope, the right shade of consideration demanded by his noble blood and his confidential position. His face cleared up in a wonderful way. It appeared that, notwithstanding my uncle's earnest assurances, the good fellow had remained in doubt of our understanding each other. He imagined I would talk to him in some foreign language. I was told that his last words on getting into the sledge to come to meet me shaped an anxious exclamation:

"Well! Well! Here I am going, but God only knows how I am to make myself understood to our master's nephew."

We understood each other very well from the first. He took charge of me as if I were not quite of age. I had a delightful boyish feeling of coming home from school when he muffled me up next morning in an enormous bear-skin travelling-coat and took his seat protectively by my side. The sledge was a very small one and it looked utterly insignificant, almost like a toy behind the four big bays harnessed two and two. We three, counting the coachman, filled it completely. He was a young fellow with clear blue eyes; the high collar of his livery fur coat framed his cheery countenance and stood all round level with the top of his head.

"Now, Joseph," my companion addressed him, "do you think we shall manage to get home before six?" His answer was that we would surely, with God's help, and providing there were no heavy drifts in the long stretch between certain villages whose names came with an extremely familiar sound to my ears. He turned out an excellent coachman with an instinct for keeping the road amongst the snow-covered fields and a natural gift of getting the best out of the horses.

"He is the son of that Joseph that I supposed the Captain remembers. He who used to drive the Captain's late grandmother of holy memory," remarked V. S. busy tucking fur rugs about my feet.

I remembered perfectly the trusty Joseph who used to drive my grandmother. Why! he it was who let me hold the reins for the first time in my life and allowed me to play with the great four-in-hand whip outside the doors of the coach-house.

"What became of him?" I asked. "He is no longer serving, I suppose."

"He served our master," was the reply. "But he died of cholera ten years ago now—that great epidemic we had. And his wife died at the same time—the whole houseful of them, and this is the only boy that was left."

The MS. of "Almayer's Folly" was reposing in the bag under our feet.

I saw again the sun setting on the plains as I saw it in the travels of my childhood. It set, clear and red, dipping into the snow in full view as if it were setting on the sea. It was twenty-three years since I had seen the sun set over that land; and we drove on in the darkness which fell swiftly upon the livid expanse of snows till, out of the waste of a white earth joining a be-starred sky, surged up black shapes, the clumps of trees about a village of the Ukrainian plain. A cottage or two glided by, a low interminable wall and then, glimmering and winking through a screen of fir-trees, the lights of the master's house.

That very evening the wandering MS. of "Almayer's Folly" was unpacked and unostentatiously laid on the writing-table in my room, the guest-room which had been, I was informed in an affectedly careless tone, awaiting me for some fifteen years or so. It attracted no attention from the affectionate presence hovering round the son of the favourite sister.

"You won't have many hours to yourself while you are staying with me, brother," he said—this form of address borrowed from the speech of our peasants being the usual expression of the highest good humour in a moment of affectionate elation. "I shall be always coming in for a chat."

As a matter of fact we had the whole house to chat in and were everlastingly intruding upon each other. I

invaded the retirement of his study, where the principal
feature was a colossal silver inkstand presented to him
on his fiftieth year by a subscription of all his wards
then living. He had been guardian of many orphans of
land-owning families from the three southern provinces
—ever since the year 1860. Some of them had been my
schoolfellows and playmates, but not one of them, girls
or boys, that I know of, has ever written a novel. One
or two were older than myself—considerably older, too.
One of them, a visitor I remember in my early years,
was the man who first put me on horseback, and his
four-horse bachelor turn-out, his perfect horsemanship
and general skill in manly exercises was one of my
earliest admirations. I seem to remember my mother
looking on from a colonnade in front of the dining-room
windows as I was lifted upon the pony, held, for all I
know, by the very Joseph—the groom attached specially
to my grandmother's service—who died of cholera. It
was certainly a young man in a dark blue, tail-less coat
and huge Cossack trousers, that being the livery of the
men about the stables. It must have been in 1864, but
reckoning by another mode of calculating time, it was
certainly in the year in which my mother obtained
permission to travel south and visit her family, from the
exile into which she had followed my father. For that,
too, she had had to ask permission, and I know that one
of the conditions of that favour was that she should be
treated exactly as a condemned exile herself. Yet a
couple of years later, in memory of her eldest brother
who had served in the Guards and dying early left hosts
of friends and a loved memory in the great world of
St. Petersburg, some influential personages procured for
her this permission—it was officially called the "Highest
Grace"—of a three months' leave from exile.

This is also the year in which I first begin to remember

my mother with more distinctness than a mere loving, wide-browed, silent, protecting presence, whose eyes had a sort of commanding sweetness; and I also remember, the great gathering of all the relations from near and far, and the grey heads of the family friends paying her the homage of respect and love in the house of her favourite brother who, a few years later, was to take the place for me of both my parents.

I did not understand the tragic significance of it all at the time, though indeed I remember that doctors also came. There were no signs of invalidism about her— but I think that already they had pronounced her doom unless perhaps the change to a southern climate could re-establish her declining strength. For me it seems the very happiest period of my existence. There was my cousin, a delightful, quick-tempered little girl, some months younger than myself, whose life, lovingly watched over, as if she were a royal princess, came to an end with her fifteenth year. There were other children too, many of whom are dead now, and not a few whose very names I have forgotten. Over all this hung the oppressive shadow of the great Russian Empire—the shadow lowering with the darkness of a new-born national hatred fostered by the Moscow school of journalists against the Poles after the ill-omened rising of 1863.

This is a far cry back from the MS. of "Almayer's Folly," but the public record of these formative impressions is not the whim of an uneasy egotism. These, too, are things human, already distant in their appeal. It is meet that something more should be left for the novelist's children than the colours and figures of his own hard-won creation. That which in their grown-up years may appear to the world about them as the most enigmatic side of their natures and perhaps must remain for ever obscure even to themselves, will be their unconscious response to the still voice of that inexorable past from which his work of fiction and their personalities are remotely derived.

—Only in men's imagination does every truth find an effective and undeniable existence. Imagination, not invention, is the supreme master of art as of life. An imaginative and exact rendering of authentic memories may serve worthily that spirit of piety towards all things human which sanctions the conceptions of a writer of tales, and the emotions of the man reviewing his own experience.

II

As I have said, I was unpacking my luggage after a journey from London into Ukraine. The MS. of "Almayer's Folly"—my companion already for some three years or more, and then in the ninth chapter of its age—was deposited unostentatiously on the writing-table placed between two windows. It didn't occur to me to put it away in the drawer the table was fitted with, but my eye was attracted by the good form of the same drawer's brass handles. Two candelabra, with four candles each, lighted up festally the room which had waited so many years for the wandering nephew. The blinds were down.

Within five hundred yards of the chair on which I sat stood the first peasant hut of the village—part of my maternal grandfather's estate, the only part remaining in the possession of a member of the family; and beyond the village in the limitless blackness of a winter's night there lay the great unfenced fields—not a flat and severe plain, but a kindly, bread-giving land of low, rounded ridges, all white now, with the black patches of timber nestling in the hollows. The road by which I had come ran through a village with a turn just outside the gates closing the short drive. Somebody was abroad on the deep snow-track; a quick tinkle of bells stole gradually into the stillness of the room like a tuneful whisper.

My unpacking had been watched over by the servant who had come to help me, and, for the most part, had been standing attentive but unnecessary at the door of the room. I did not want him in the least, but I did not like to tell him to go away. He was a young fellow, certainly more than ten years younger than myself; I had not been—I won't say in that place but within sixty miles of it, ever since the year '67; yet his guileless physiognomy of the open peasant type seemed strangely familiar. It was quite possible that he might have been a descendant, a son or even a grandson, of the servants whose friendly faces had been familiar to me in my early childhood. As a matter of fact he had no such claim on my consideration. He was the product of some village near by and was there on his promotion, having learned the service in one or two houses as pantry-boy. I know this because I asked the worthy V—— next day. I might well have spared the question. I discovered before long that all the faces about the house and all the faces in the village: the grave faces with long moustaches of the heads of families, the downy faces of the young men, the faces of the little fair-haired children, the handsome, tanned, wide-browed faces of the mothers seen at the doors of the huts, were as familiar to me as though I had known them all from childhood, and my childhood were a matter of the day before yesterday.

The tinkle of the traveller's bells, after growing louder, had faded away quickly, and the tumult of barking dogs in the village had calmed down at last. My uncle, lounging in the corner of a small couch, smoked his long Turkish *chibouk* in silence.

"This is an extremely nice writing-table you have got for my room," I remarked.

"It is really your property," he said, keeping his eyes on me, with an interested and wistful expression, as he had done ever since I had entered the house. "Forty years ago your mother used to write at this very table.

In our house in Oratow it stood in the little sitting-room which, by a tacit arrangement, was given up to the girls—I mean to your mother and her sister who died so young. It was a present to them jointly from our uncle Nicholas B. when your mother was seventeen and your aunt two years younger. She was a very dear, delightful girl, that aunt of yours, of whom I suppose you know nothing more than the name. She did not shine so much by personal beauty and a cultivated mind, in which your mother was far superior. It was her good sense, the admirable sweetness of her nature, her exceptional facility and ease in daily relations that endeared her to everybody. Her death was a terrible grief and a serious moral loss for us all. Had she lived she would have brought the greatest blessings to the house it would have been her lot to enter, as wife, mother and mistress of a household. She would have created round herself an atmosphere of peace and content which only those who can love unselfishly are able to evoke. Your mother—of far greater beauty, exceptionally distinguished in person, manner and intellect—had a less easy disposition. Being more brilliantly gifted, she also expected more from life. At that trying time, especially, we were greatly concerned about her state. Suffering in her health from the shock of her father's death (she was alone in the house with him when he died suddenly), she was torn by the inward struggle between her love for the man whom she was to marry in the end and her knowledge of her dead father's declared objection to that match. Unable to bring herself to disregard that cherished memory and that judgment she had always respected and trusted, and, on the other hand, feeling the impossibility to resist a sentiment so deep and so true, she could not have been expected to preserve her mental and moral bal-

ance. At war with herself, she could not give to others
that feeling of peace which was not her own. It was
only later, when united at last with the man of her
choice, that she developed those uncommon gifts of
mind and heart which compelled the respect and admiration even of our foes. Meeting with calm forti-
tude the cruel trials of a life reflecting all the national
and social misfortunes of the community, she realised
the highest conceptions of duty as a wife, a mother
and a patriot, sharing the exile of her husband and
representing nobly the ideal of Polish womanhood.
Our Uncle Nicholas was not a man very accessible to
feelings of affection. Apart from his worship for
Napoleon the Great, he loved really, I believe, only
three people in the world: his mother—your great-
grandmother, whom you have seen but cannot possibly
remember; his brother, our father, in whose house he
lived for so many years; and of all of us, his nephews
and nieces grown up around him, your mother alone.
The modest, lovable qualities of the youngest sister he
did not seem able to see. It was I who felt most profoundly this unexpected stroke of death falling upon the
family less than a year after I had become its head. It
was terribly unexpected. Driving home one wintry
afternoon to keep me company in our empty house,
where I had to remain permanently administering the
estate and attending to the complicated affairs—the
girls took it in turn week and week about—driving, as
I said, from the house of the Countess Tekla Potocka,
where our invalid mother was staying then to be near a
doctor, they lost the road and got stuck in a snowdrift.
She was alone with the coachman and old Valery, the
personal servant of our late father. Impatient of delay while they were trying to dig themselves out, she
jumped out of the sledge and went to look for the road

herself. All this happened in '51, not ten miles from the house in which we are sitting now. The road was soon found, but snow had begun to fall thickly again, and they were four more hours getting home. Both the men took off their sheepskin-lined great-coats and used all their own rugs to wrap her up against the cold, notwithstanding her protests, positive orders and even struggles, as Valery afterwards related to me. 'How could I,' he remonstrated with her, 'go to meet the blessed soul of my late master if I let any harm come to you while there's a spark of life left in my body?' When they reached home, at last, the poor old man was stiff and speechless from exposure, and the coachman was in not much better plight, though he had the strength to drive round to the stables himself. To my reproaches for venturing out at all in such weather, she answered characteristically that she could not bear the thought of abandoning me to my cheerless solitude. It is incomprehensible how it was that she was allowed to start. I suppose it had to be! She made light of the cough which came on next day, but shortly afterwards inflammation of the lungs set in, and in three weeks she was no more! She was the first to be taken away of the young generation under my care. Behold the vanity of all hopes and fears! I was the most frail at birth of all the children. For years I remained so delicate that my parents had but little hope of bringing me up; and yet I have survived five brothers and two sisters, and many of my contemporaries; I have outlived my wife and daughter, too—and from all those who have had some knowledge at least of these old times, you alone are left. It has been my lot to lay in an early grave many honest hearts, many brilliant promises, many hopes full of life."

He got up brusquely, sighed, and left me, saying:

"We will dine in half an hour." Without moving, I listened to his quick steps resounding on the waxed floor of the next room, traversing the ante-room lined with bookshelves, where he paused to put his *chibouk* in the pipe-stand before passing into the drawing-room (these were all *en suite*), where he became inaudible on the thick carpet. But I heard the door of his study-bedroom close. He was then sixty-two years old and had been for a quarter of a century the wisest, the firmest, the most indulgent of guardians, extending over me a paternal care and affection, a moral support which I seemed to feel always near me in the most distant parts of the earth.

As to Mr. Nicholas B., sub-lieutenant of 1808, lieutenant of 1813 in the French Army, and for a short time *Officier d'Ordonnance* of Marshal Marmont; afterwards Captain in the 2nd Regiment of Mounted Rifles in the Polish Army—such as it existed up to 1830 in the reduced kingdom established by the Congress of Vienna —I must say that from all that more distant past, known to me traditionally and a little *de visu*, and called out by the words of the man just gone away, he remains the most incomplete figure. It is obvious that I must have seen him in '64, for it is certain that he would not have missed the opportunity of seeing my mother for what he must have known would be the last time. From my early boyhood to this day, if I try to call up his image, a sort of mist rises before my eyes, a mist in which I perceive vaguely only a neatly brushed head of white hair (which is exceptional in the case of the B. family, where it is the rule for men to go bald in a becoming manner, before thirty) and a thin, curved, dignified nose, a feature in strict accordance with the physical tradition of the B. family. But it is not by these fragmentary remains of perishable mortality that he lives in my memory. I knew, at a very early age, that my grand-uncle Nicholas B. was a Knight of the Legion of Honour and that he had also the Polish Cross for valour, *Virtuti Militari*. The knowledge of these glorious facts inspired in me an admiring veneration; yet it is not that sentiment, strong as it was, which resumes for me the force and the significance of his personality. It is overborne by another and complex impression of awe, compassion and horror. Mr. Nicholas B. remains for me the unfortunate and miserable (but heroic) being who once upon a time had eaten a dog.

It is a good forty years since I heard the tale, and the effect has not worn off yet. I believe this is the very first, say, realistic, story I heard in my life; but all the same, I don't know why I should have been so frightfully impressed. Of course I know what our village dogs look like—but still . . . No! At this very day, recalling the horror and compassion of my childhood, I ask myself whether I am right in disclosing to a cold and fastidious world that awful episode in the family history. I ask myself—is it right?—especially as the B. family had always been honourably known in a wide country-side for the delicacy of their tastes in the matter of eating and drinking. But upon the whole, and considering that this gastronomical degradation overtaking a gallant young officer lies really at the door of the Great Napoleon, I think that to cover it up by silence would be an exaggeration of literary restraint. Let the truth stand here. The responsibility rests with the Man of St. Helena in view of his deplorable levity in the conduct of the Russian campaign. It was during the memorable retreat from Moscow that Mr. Nicholas B., in company of two brother officers—as to whose morality and natural refinement I know nothing—

bagged a dog on the outskirts of a village and subsequently devoured him. As far as I can remember, the weapon used was a cavalry sabre, and the issue of the sporting episode was rather more of a matter of life and death than if it had been an encounter with a tiger. A picket of Cossacks was sleeping in that village lost in the depths of the great Lithuanian forest. The three sportsmen had observed them from a hiding-place making themselves very much at home amongst the huts just before the early winter darkness set in at four o'clock. They had observed them with disgust and perhaps with despair. Late in the night the rash counsels of hunger overcame the dictates of prudence. Crawling through the snow, they crept up to the fence of dry branches which generally encloses a village in that part of Lithuania. What they expected to get, and in what manner, and whether this expectation was worth the risk, goodness only knows. However, these Cossack parties in most cases wandering without an officer, were known to guard themselves badly and often not at all. In addition, the village lying at a great distance from the line of French retreat, they could not suspect the presence of stragglers from the Grand Army. The three officers had strayed away in a blizzard from the main column and had been lost for days in the woods, which explains sufficiently the terrible straits to which they were reduced. Their plan was to try and attract the attention of the peasants in that one of the huts which was nearest to the enclosure; but as they were preparing to venture into the very jaws of the lion, so to speak, a dog (it is mighty strange that there was but one), a creature quite as formidable under the circumstances as a lion, began to bark on the other side of the fence . . . .

At this stage of the narrative, which I heard many

times (by request) from the lips of Captain Nicholas
B.'s sister-in-law, my grandmother, I used to tremble
with excitement.

The dog barked. And if he had done no more than
bark, three officers of the Great Napoleon's army would
have perished honourably on the points of Cossacks'
lances, or perchance escaping the chase, would have
died decently of starvation. But before they had time
to think of running away, that fatal and revolting dog,
being carried away by the excess of his zeal, dashed
out through a gap in the fence. He dashed out and
died. His head, I understand, was severed at one
blow from his body. I understand also that, later on,
within the gloomy solitudes of the snow-laden woods,
when in a sheltering hollow, a fire had been lit by the
party, the condition of the quarry was discovered to be
distinctly unsatisfactory. It was not thin—on the
contrary, it seemed unhealthily obese; its skin showed
bare patches of an unpleasant character. However,
they had not killed that dog for the sake of the pelt.
He was large. . . . He was eaten. . . . The
rest is silence . . . A silence in which a small boy
shudders and says firmly:

"I could not have eaten that dog."

And his grandmother remarks with a smile:

"Perhaps you don't know what it is to be hungry."

I have learned something of it since. Not that I have
been reduced to eat dog. I have fed on the emble-
matical animal, which, in the language of the volatile
Gauls, is called *la vache enragée;* I have lived on ancient
salt junk, I know the taste of shark, of trepang, of snake,
of nondescript dishes containing things without a
name—but of the Lithuanian village dog, never! I
wish it to be distinctly understood that it is not I, but
my grand-uncle Nicholas, of the Polish landed gentry,

Chevalier de la Légion d'Honneur, etc. etc., who, in his young days, had eaten the Lithuanian dog.

I wish he had not. The childish horror of the deed clings absurdly to the grizzled man. I am perfectly helpless against it. Still, if he really had to, let us charitably remember that he had eaten him on active service, while bearing up bravely against the greatest military disaster of modern history, and, in a manner, for the sake of his country. He had eaten him to appease his hunger, no doubt, but also for the sake of an unappeasable and patriotic desire, in the glow of a great faith that lives still, and in the pursuit of a great illusion kindled like a false beacon by a great man to lead astray the effort of a brave nation.

Pro patria !

Looked at in that light it appears a sweet and decorous meal.

And looked at in the same light, my own diet of *la vache enragée* appears a fatuous and extravagant form of self-indulgence; for why should I, the son of a land which such men as these have turned up with their ploughshares and bedewed with their blood, undertake the pursuit of fantastic meals of salt junk and hard tack upon the wide seas? On the kindest view it seems an unanswerable question. Alas! I have the conviction that there are men of unstained rectitude who are ready to murmur scornfully the word desertion. Thus the taste of innocent adventure may be made bitter to the palate. The part of the inexplicable should be allowed for in appraising the conduct of men in a world where no explanation is final. No charge of faithlessness ought to be lightly uttered. The appearances of this perishable life are deceptive like everything that falls under the judgment of our imperfect senses. The inner voice may remain true enough in its secret counsel. The fidelity to a special tradition may last through the events of an unrelated existence, following faithfully, too, the traced way of an inexplicable impulse.

It would take too long to explain the intimate alliance of contradictions in human nature which makes love itself wear at times the desperate shape of betrayal. And perhaps there is no possible explanation. Indulgence—as somebody said—is the most intelligent of all the virtues. I venture to think that it is one of the least common, if not the most uncommon of all. I would not imply by this that men are foolish—or even most men. Far from it. The barber and the priest, backed by the whole opinion of the village, condemned justly the conduct of the ingenious hidalgo who, sallying forth from his native place, broke the head of the muleteer, put to death a flock of inoffensive sheep, and went through very doleful experiences in a certain stable. God forbid that an unworthy churl should escape merited censure by hanging on to the stirrup-leather of the sublime *caballero*. His was a very noble, a very unselfish fantasy, fit for nothing except to raise the envy of baser mortals. But there is more than one aspect to the charm of that exalted and dangerous figure. He, too, had his frailties. After reading so many romances he desired naïvely to escape with his very body from the intolerable reality of things. He wished to meet eye to eye the valorous giant Brandabarbaran, Lord of Arabia, whose armour is made of the skin of a dragon, and whose shield, strapped to his arm, is the gate of a fortified city. O amiable and natural weakness! O blessed simplicity of a gentle heart without guile! Who would not succumb to such a consoling temptation? Nevertheless it was a form of self-indulgence, and the ingenious hidalgo of La Mancha was not a good citizen. The priest and the barber were not unreasonable in their strictures. Without going so far as the old King Louis-Philippe, who used to say in his exile, "The people are never in fault"—one may admit that there must be some righteousness in the assent of a whole village. Mad! Mad! He who kept in pious meditation the ritual vigil-of-arms by the well of an inn and knelt reverently to be knighted at daybreak by the fat, sly rogue of a landlord, has come very near perfection. He rides forth, his head encircled by a halo—the patron saint of all lives spoiled or saved by the irresistible grace of imagination. But he was not a good citizen.

Perhaps that and nothing else was meant by the well-remembered exclamation of my tutor.

It was in the jolly year 1873, the very last year in which I have had a jolly holiday. There have been idle years afterwards, jolly enough in a way and not altogether without their lesson, but this year of which I speak was the year of my last schoolboy holiday. There are other reasons why I should remember that year, but they are too long to state formally in this place. Moreover they have nothing to do with that holiday. What has to do with the holiday is that before the day on which the remark was made we had seen Vienna, the Upper Danube, Munich, the Falls of the Rhine, the Lake of Constance—in fact it was a memorable holiday of travel. Of late we had been tramping slowly up the Valley of the Reuss. It was a delightful time. It was much more like a stroll than a tramp. Landing from a Lake of Lucerne steamer in Fluellen, we found ourselves at the end of the second day, with the dusk overtaking our leisurely footsteps, a little way beyond Hospenthal. This is not the day on which the remark was made: in the shadows of the

deep valley and with the habitations of men left some
way behind, our thoughts ran not upon the ethics of
conduct but upon the simpler human problem of shelter
and food.   There did not seem anything of the kind
in sight, and we were thinking of turning back when
suddenly at a bend of the road we came upon a building,
ghostly in the twilight.

At that time the work on the St. Gothard Tunnel
was going on, and that magnificent enterprise of burrow-
ing was directly responsible for the unexpected building
standing all alone upon the very roots of the mountains.
It was long, though not big at all; it was low; it was
built of boards, without ornamentation, in barrack hut
style, with the white window-frames quite flush with
the yellow face of its plain front.   And yet it was an
hotel; it had even a name which I have forgotten.   But
there was no gold-laced door-keeper at its humble door.
A plain but vigorous servant-girl answered our inquiries, then a man and woman who owned the place
appeared.   It was clear that no travellers were expected, or perhaps even desired, in this strange hostelry,
which in its severe style resembled the house which
surmounts the unseaworthy-looking hulls of the toy
Noah's Arks, the universal possession of European
childhood.   However, its roof was not hinged and it
was not full to the brim of slab-sided and painted
animals of wood.   Even the live tourist animal was
nowhere in evidence.   We had something to eat in a
long, narrow room at one end of a long, narrow table,
which, to my tired perception and to my sleepy eyes,
seemed as if it would tilt up like a see-saw plank, since
there was no one at the other end to balance it against
our two dusty and travel-stained figures.   Then we hastened upstairs to bed in a room smelling of pine planks,
and I was fast asleep before my head touched the pillow.

In the morning my tutor (he was a student of the Cracow University) woke me up early, and as we were dressing remarked: "There seems to be a lot of people staying in this hotel. I have heard a noise of talking up till eleven o'clock." This statement surprised me; I had heard no noise whatever, having slept like a top.

We went downstairs into the long and narrow dining-room with its long and narrow table. There were two rows of plates on it. At one of the many uncurtained windows stood a tall, bony man with a bald head set off by a bunch of black hair above each ear and with a long black beard. He glanced up from the paper he was reading and seemed genuinely astonished at our intrusion. By and by more men came in. Not one of them looked like a tourist. Not a single woman appeared. These men seemed to know each other with some intimacy, but I cannot say they were a very talkative lot. The bald-headed man sat down gravely at the head of the table. It all had the air of a family party. By and by, from one of the vigorous servant-girls in national costume, we discovered that the place was really a boarding-house for some English engineers engaged at the works of the St. Gothard Tunnel; and I could listen my fill to the sounds of the English language as far as it is used at a breakfast-table by men who do not believe in wasting many words on the mere amenities of life.

This was my first contact with British mankind apart from the tourist kind seen in the hotels of Zurich and Lucerne—the kind which has no real existence in a workaday world. I know now that the bald-headed man spoke with a strong Scotch accent. I have met many of his kind since, both ashore and afloat. The second engineer of the steamer *Mavis*, for instance, ought to have been his twin brother. I cannot help thinking that he really was, though for some reasons of his own he assured me that he never had a twin brother. Anyway, the deliberate, bald-headed Scot with the coal-black beard appeared to my boyish eyes a very romantic and mysterious person.

We slipped out unnoticed. Our mapped-out route led over the Furca Pass towards the Rhône Glacier, with the further intention of following down the trend of the Häsli Valley. The sun was already declining when we found ourselves on the top of the pass, and the remark alluded to was presently uttered.

We sat down by the side of the road to continue the argument begun half a mile or so before. I am certain it was an argument because I remember perfectly how my tutor argued and how without the power of reply I listened with my eyes fixed obstinately on the ground. A stir on the road made me look up—and then I saw my unforgettable Englishman. There are acquaintances of later years, familiars, shipmates, whom I remember less clearly. He marched rapidly towards the east (attended by a hang-dog Swiss guide) with the mien of an ardent and fearless traveller. He was clad in a knickerbocker suit, but as at the same time he wore short socks under his laced boots, for reasons which, whether hygienic or conscientious, were surely imaginative, his calves exposed to the public gaze and to the tonic air of high altitudes, dazzled the beholder by the splendour of their marble-like condition and their rich tone of young ivory. He was the leader of a small caravan. The light of a headlong, exalted satisfaction with the world of men and the scenery of mountains illumined his clean-cut, very red face, his short, silver-white whiskers, his innocently eager and triumphant eyes. In passing he cast a glance of kindly curiosity and a friendly gleam of big, sound, shiny teeth towards the man and the boy sitting like dusty tramps by the roadside, with a modest knapsack lying at their feet. His white calves twinkled sturdily, the uncouth Swiss guide with a surly mouth stalked like an unwilling bear at his elbow; a small train of three mules followed in single file the lead of this inspiring enthusiast. Two ladies rode past one behind the other, but from the way they sat I only saw their calm, uniform backs, and the long ends of blue veils hanging behind far down over their identical hat-brims. His two daughters, surely. An industrious luggage-mule, with unstarched ears and guarded by a slouching, sallow driver, brought up the rear. My tutor, after pausing for a look and a faint smile, resumed his earnest argument.

I tell you it was a memorable year! One does not meet such an Englishman twice in a lifetime. Was he in the mystic ordering of common events the ambassador of my future, sent out to turn the scale at a critical moment on the top of an Alpine pass, with the peaks of the Bernese Oberland for mute and solemn witnesses? His glance, his smile, the unextinguishable and comic ardour of his striving-forward appearance helped me to pull myself together. It must be stated that on that day and in the exhilarating atmosphere of that elevated spot I had been feeling utterly crushed. It was the year in which I had first spoken aloud of my desire to go to sea. At first, like those sounds that, ranging outside the scale to which men's ears are attuned, remain inaudible to our sense of hearing, this declaration passed unperceived. It was as if it had not been. Later on, by trying various tones, I managed to arouse here and there a surprised momentary attention—the "What was that funny noise?" sort of inquiry. Later on it was—"Did you hear what that boy said? What an extraordinary outbreak!" Presently a wave of scandalised astonishment (it could not have been greater if I had announced the intention of entering a Carthusian monastery) ebbing out of the educational and academical town of Cracow spread itself over several provinces. It spread itself shallow but far-reaching. It stirred up a mass of remonstrance, indignation, pitying wonder, bitter irony and downright chaff. I could hardly breathe under its weight, and certainly had no words for an answer. People wondered what Mr. T. B. would do now with his worrying nephew and, I dare say, hoped kindly that he would make short work of my nonsense.

What he did was to come down all the way from Ukraine to have it out with me and to judge by himself, unprejudiced, impartial and just, taking his stand on the ground of wisdom and affection. As far as is possible for a boy whose power of expression is still unformed, I opened the secret of my thoughts to him and he in return allowed me a glimpse into his mind and heart; the first glimpse of an inexhaustible and noble treasure of clear thought and warm feeling, which through life was to be mine to draw upon with a never-deceived love and confidence. Practically, after several exhaustive conversations, he concluded that he would not have me later on reproach him for having spoiled my life by an unconditional opposition. But I must take time for serious reflection. And I must not only think of myself but of others; weigh the claims of affection and conscience against my own sincerity of purpose. "Think well what it all means in the larger issues, my boy," he exhorted me finally with special friendliness. "And meantime try to get the best place you can at the yearly examinations."

The scholastic year came to an end. I took a fairly good place at the exams, which for me (for certain

reasons) happened to be a more difficult task than for
other boys. In that respect I could enter with a good
conscience upon that holiday which was like a long
visit *pour prendre congé* of the mainland of old Europe
I was to see so little of for the next four-and-twenty
years. Such, however, was not the avowed purpose of
that tour. It was rather, I suspect, planned in order
to distract and occupy my thoughts in other directions.
Nothing had been said for months of my going to sea.
But my attachment to my young tutor and his influence
over me were so well known that he must have received
a confidential mission to talk me out of my romantic
folly. It was an excellently appropriate arrangement, as
neither he nor I had ever had a single glimpse of the sea
in our lives. That was to come by and by for both
of us in Venice, from the outer shore of Lido. Meantime he had taken his mission to heart so well that I
began to feel crushed before we reached Zurich. He
argued in railway trains, in lake steamboats, he had
argued away for me the obligatory sunrise on the Rigi,
by Jove! Of his devotion to his unworthy pupil there
can be no doubt. He had proved it already by two
years of unremitting and arduous care. I could not
hate him. But he had been crushing me slowly, and
when he started to argue on the top of the Furca Pass
he was perhaps nearer a success than either he or I
imagined. I listened to him in despairing silence, feeling that ghostly, unrealised and desired sea of my
dreams escape from the unnerved grip of my will.

The enthusiastic old Englishman had passed—and
the argument went on. What reward could I expect
from such a life at the end of my years, either in ambition, honour or conscience? An unanswerable question. But I felt no longer crushed. Then our eyes
met and a genuine emotion was visible in his as well as

in mine. The end came all at once. He picked up the knapsack suddenly and got on to his feet.

"You are an incorrigible, hopeless Don Quixote. That's what you are."

I was surprised. I was only fifteen and did not know what he meant exactly. But I felt vaguely flattered at the name of the immortal knight turning up in connection with my own folly, as some people would call it to my face. Alas! I don't think there was anything to be proud of. Mine was not the stuff the protectors of forlorn damsels, the redressers of this world's wrongs are made of; and my tutor was the man to know that best. Therein, in his indignation, he was superior to the barber and the priest when he flung at me an honoured name like a reproach.

I walked behind him for full five minutes; then without looking back he stopped. The shadows of distant peaks were lengthening over the Furca Pass. When I came up to him he turned to me and in full view of the Finster-Aarhorn, with his band of giant brothers rearing their monstrous heads against a brilliant sky, put his hand on my shoulder affectionately.

"Well! That's enough. We will have no more of it."

And indeed there was no more question of my mysterious vocation between us. There was to be no more question of it at all, nowhere or with any one. We began the descent of the Furca Pass conversing merrily. Eleven years later, month for month, I stood on Tower Hill on the steps of the St. Katherine's Dockhouse, a master in the British Merchant Service. But the man who put his hand on my shoulder at the top of the Furca Pass was no longer living.

That very year of our travels he took his degree of the Philosophical Faculty—and only then his true vocation declared itself. Obedient to the call, he entered at once upon the four-year course of the Medical Schools. A day came when, on the deck of a ship moored in Calcutta, I opened a letter telling me of the end of an enviable existence. He had made for himself a practice in some obscure little town of Austrian Galicia. And the letter went on to tell me how all the bereaved poor of the district, Christians and Jews alike, had mobbed the good doctor's coffin with sobs and lamentations at the very gate of the cemetery.

How short his years and how clear his vision! What greater reward in ambition, honour and conscience could he have hoped to win for himself when, on the top of the Furca Pass, he bade me look well to the end of my opening life.

III

THE devouring in a dismal forest of a luckless Lithuanian dog by my grand-uncle Nicholas B. in company
of two other military and famished scarecrows, sym-
bolised, to my childish imagination, the whole horror
of the retreat from Moscow and the immorality of a
conqueror's ambition. An extreme distaste for that
objectionable episode has tinged the views I hold as to
the character and achievements of Napoleon the Great.
I need not say that these are unfavourable. It was
morally reprehensible for that great captain to induce a
simple-minded Polish gentleman to eat dog by raising
in his breast a false hope of national independence. It
has been the fate of that credulous nation to starve for
upwards of a hundred years on a diet of false hopes and
—well—dog. It is, when one thinks of it, a singularly
poisonous regimen. Some pride in the national con-
stitution which has survived a long course of such
dishes is really excusable. But enough of generalising.
Returning to particulars, Mr. Nicholas B. confided to
his sister-in-law (my grandmother) in his misanthropi-
cally laconic manner that this supper in the woods had
been nearly "the death of him." This is not surprising.
What surprises me is that the story was ever heard of;
for grand-uncle Nicholas differed in this from the
generality of military men of Napoleon's time (and perhaps of all time), that he did not like to talk of his
campaigns, which began at Friedland and ended somewhere in the neighbourhood of Bar-le-Duc. His admiration of the great Emperor was unreserved in

everything but expression. Like the religion of earnest men, it was too profound a sentiment to be displayed before a world of little faith. Apart from that he seemed as completely devoid of military anecdotes as though he had hardly ever seen a soldier in his life. Proud of his decorations, earned before he was twenty-five, he refused to wear the ribbons at the buttonhole in the manner practised to this day in Europe and even was unwilling to display the insignia on festive occasions, as though he wished to conceal them in the fear of appearing boastful. "It is enough that I have them," he used to mutter. In the course of thirty years they were seen on his breast only twice—at an auspicious marriage in the family and at the funeral of an old friend. That the wedding which was thus honoured was not the wedding of my mother, I learned only late in life, too late to bear a grudge against Mr. Nicholas B., who made amends at my birth by a long letter of congratulation containing the following prophecy: "He will see better times." Even in his embittered heart there lived a hope. But he was not a true prophet.

He was a man of strange contradictions. Living for many years in his brother's house, the home of many children, a house full of life, of animation, noisy with a constant coming and going of many guests, he kept his habits of solitude and silence. Considered as obstinately secretive in all his purposes, he was in reality the victim of a most painful irresolution in all matters of civil life. Under his taciturn, phlegmatic behaviour was hidden a faculty of short-lived, passionate anger. I suspect he had no talent for narrative; but it seemed to afford him sombre satisfaction to declare that he was the last man to ride over the bridge of the river Elster after the battle of Leipsic. Lest some construction favourable to his valour should be put on the fact, he condescended to explain how it came to pass. It seems that shortly after the retreat began he was sent back to the town where some divisions of the French Army (and amongst them the Polish corps of Prince Joseph Poniatowski), jammed hopelessly in the streets, were being simply exterminated by the troops of the Allied Powers. When asked what it was like in there, Mr. Nicholas B. muttered the only word "Shambles." Having delivered his message to the Prince he hastened away at once to render an account of his mission to the superior who had sent him. By that time the advance of the enemy had enveloped the town, and he was shot at from houses and chased all the way to the river bank by a disorderly mob of Austrian Dragoons and Prussian Hussars. The bridge had been mined early in the morning and his opinion was that the sight of the horsemen converging from many sides in the pursuit of his person alarmed the officer in command of the sappers and caused the premature firing of the charges. He had not gone more than 200 yards on the other side when he heard the sound of the fatal explosions. Mr. Nicholas B. concluded his bald narrative with the word "Imbecile," uttered with the utmost deliberation. It testified to his indignation at the loss of so many thousands of lives. But his phlegmatic physiognomy lighted up when he spoke of his only wound, with something resembling satisfaction. You will see that there was some reason for it when you learn that he was wounded in the heel. "Like his Majesty the Emperor Napoleon himself," he reminded his hearers with assumed indifference. There can be no doubt that the indifference was assumed if one thinks what a very distinguished sort of wound it was. In all the history of warfare there are, I believe, only three warriors

publicly known to have been wounded in the heel—
Achilles and Napoleon—demigods indeed—to whom the
familial piety of an unworthy descendant adds the
name of the simple mortal, Nicholas B.

The Hundred Days found Mr. Nicholas B. staying
with a distant relative of ours, owner of a small estate in
Galicia. How he got there across the breadth of an
armed Europe and after what adventures I am afraid
will never be known now. All his papers were destroyed shortly before his death; but if there was
amongst them, as he affirmed, a concise record of his
life, then I am pretty sure it did not take up more than
a half-sheet of foolscap or so. This relative of ours
happened to be an Austrian officer, who had left the
service after the battle of Austerlitz. Unlike Mr.
Nicholas B., who concealed his decorations, he liked to
display his honourable discharge in which he was
mentioned as *unschreckbar* (fearless) before the enemy.
No conjunction could seem more unpromising, yet it
stands in the family tradition that these two got on very
well together in their rural solitude.

When asked whether he had not been sorely tempted
during the Hundred Days to make his way again to
France and join the service of his beloved Emperor,
Mr. Nicholas B. used to mutter: "No money. No
horse. Too far to walk."

The fall of Napoleon and the ruin of national hopes
affected adversely the character of Mr. Nicholas B.
He shrank from returning to his province. But for that
there was also another reason. Mr. Nicholas B. and
his brother—my maternal grandfather—had lost their
father early, while they were quite children. Their
mother, young still and left very well off, married again
a man of great charm and of an amiable disposition but
without a penny. He turned out an affectionate and

careful stepfather; it was unfortunate though that while
directing the boys' education and forming their character by wise counsel he did his best to get hold of the
fortune by buying and selling land in his own name and
investing capital in such a manner as to cover up the
traces of the real ownership. It seems that such
practices can be successful if one is charming enough to
dazzle one's own wife permanently and brave enough to
defy the vain terrors of public opinion. The critical
time came when the elder of the boys on attaining his
majority in the year 1811 asked for the accounts and
some part at least of the inheritance to begin life upon.
It was then that the stepfather declared with calm
finality that there were no accounts to render and no
property to inherit. The whole fortune was his very
own. He was very good-natured about the young
man's misapprehension of the true state of affairs, but
of course felt obliged to maintain his position firmly.
Old friends came and went busily, voluntary mediators
appeared travelling on most horrible roads from the
most distant corners of the three provinces; and the
Marshal of the Nobility (*ex-officio* guardian of all well-
born orphans) called a meeting of landowners to
"ascertain in a friendly way how the misunderstanding
between X and his stepsons had arisen and devise
proper measures to remove the same." A deputation to
that effect visited X, who treated them to excellent
wines, but absolutely refused his ear to their remonstrances. As to the proposals for arbitration he simply
laughed at them; yet the whole province must have
been aware that fourteen years before, when he married
the widow, all his visible fortune consisted (apart from
his social qualities) in a smart four-horse turn-out with
two servants, with whom he went about visiting from
house to house; and as to any funds he might have pos-

sessed at that time their existence could only be inferred
from the fact that he was very punctual in settling his
modest losses at cards. But by the magic power of stub-
born and constant assertion, there were found presently,
here and there, people who mumbled that surely "there
must be something in it." However, on his next name-
day (which he used to celebrate by a great three-days'
shooting-party), of all the invited crowd only two guests
turned up, distant neighbours of no importance; one
notoriously a fool, and the other a very pious and honest
person but such a passionate lover of the gun that on his
own confession he could not have refused an invitation
to a shooting-party from the devil himself. X met this
manifestation of public opinion with the serenity of an
unstained conscience. He refused to be crushed. Yet
he must have been a man of deep feeling, because, when
his wife took openly the part of her children, he lost his
beautiful tranquillity, proclaimed himself heart-broken
and drove her out of the house, neglecting in his grief to
give her enough time to pack her trunks.

This was the beginning of a lawsuit, an abominable
marvel of chicane, which by the use of every legal
subterfuge was made to last for many years. It was
also the occasion for a display of much kindness and
sympathy. All the neighbouring houses flew open for
the reception of the homeless. Neither legal aid nor
material assistance in the prosecution of the suit was
ever wanting. X, on his side, went about shedding
tears publicly over his stepchildren's ingratitude and
his wife's blind infatuation; but as at the same time
he displayed great cleverness in the art of concealing
material documents (he was even suspected of having
burnt a lot of historically interesting family papers),
this scandalous litigation had to be ended by a com-
promise lest worse should befall. It was settled finally

by a surrender, out of the disputed estate, in full satisfaction of all claims, of two villages with the names of which I do not intend to trouble my readers. After this lame and impotent conclusion neither the wife nor the stepsons had anything to say to the man who had presented the world with such a successful example of self-help based on character, determination and industry; and my great-grandmother, her health completely broken down, died a couple of years later in Carlsbad. Legally secured by a decree in the possession of his plunder, X regained his wonted serenity and went on living in the neighbourhood in a comfortable style and in apparent peace of mind. His big shoots were fairly well attended again. He was never tired of assuring people that he bore no grudge for what was past; he protested loudly of his constant affection for his wife and step-children. It was true, he said, that they had tried their best to strip him as naked as a Turkish saint in the decline of his days; and because he had defended himself from spoliation, as anybody else in his place would have done, they had abandoned him now to the horrors of a solitary old age. Nevertheless, his love for them survived these cruel blows. And there might have been some truth in his protestations. Very soon he began to make overtures of friendship to his eldest stepson, my maternal grandfather; and when these were peremptorily rejected, he went on renewing them again and again with characteristic obstinacy. For years he persisted in his efforts at reconciliation, promising my grandfather to execute a will in his favour if he only would be friends again to the extent of calling now and then (it was fairly close neighbourhood for these parts, forty miles or so), or even of putting in an appearance for the great shoot on the name-day. My grandfather was an ardent lover of every sport. His temperament was as free from hardness and animosity as can be imagined. Pupil of the liberal-minded Benedictines who directed the only public school of some standing then in the south, he had also read deeply the authors of the eighteenth century. In him Christian charity was joined to a philosophical indulgence for the failings of human nature. But the memory of these miserably anxious early years, his young man's years robbed of all generous illusions by the cynicism of the sordid lawsuit, stood in the way of forgiveness. He never succumbed to the fascination of the great shoot; and X, his heart set to the last on reconciliation with the draft of the will ready for signature kept by his bed-side, died intestate. The fortune thus acquired and augmented by a wise and careful management passed to some distant relatives whom he had never seen and who even did not bear his name.

Meantime the blessing of general peace descended upon Europe. Mr. Nicholas B. bidding good-bye to his hospitable relative, the "fearless" Austrian officer, departed from Galicia, and without going near his native place, where the odious lawsuit was still going on, proceeded straight to Warsaw and entered the army of the newly constituted Polish kingdom under the sceptre of Alexander I., Autocrat of all the Russias.

This Kingdom, created by the Vienna Congress as an acknowledgment to a nation of its former independent existence, included only the central provinces of the old Polish patrimony. A brother of the Emperor, the Grand Duke Constantine (Pavlovitch), its Viceroy and Commander-in-Chief, married morganatically to a Polish lady to whom he was fiercely attached, extended this affection to what he called "My Poles" in a capricious and savage manner. Sallow in complexion, with a Tartar physiognomy and fierce little eyes, he walked with his fists clenched, his body bent forward, darting suspicious glances from under an enormous cocked hat. His intelligence was limited and his sanity itself was doubtful. The hereditary taint expressed itself, in his case, not by mystic leanings as in his two brothers, Alexander and Nicholas (in their various ways, for one was mystically liberal and the other mystically autocratic), but by the fury of an uncontrollable temper which generally broke out in disgusting abuse on the parade ground. He was a passionate militarist and an amazing drill-master. He treated his Polish Army as a spoiled child treats a favourite toy, except that he did not take it to bed with him at night. It was not small enough for that. But he played with it all day and every day, delighting in the variety of pretty uniforms and in the fun of incessant drilling. This childish passion, not for war but for mere militarism, achieved a desirable result. The Polish Army, in its equipment, in its armament and in its battlefield efficiency, as then understood, became, by the end of the year 1830, a first-rate tactical instrument. Polish peasantry (not serfs) served in the ranks by enlistment, and the officers belonged mainly to the smaller nobility. Mr. Nicholas B., with his Napoleonic record, had no difficulty in obtaining a lieutenancy, but the promotion in the Polish Army was slow, because, being a separate organisation, it took no part in the wars of the Russian Empire either against Persia or Turkey. Its first campaign, against Russia itself, was to be its last. In 1831, on the outbreak of the Revolution, Mr. Nicholas B. was the senior captain of his regiment. Some time before he had been made head of the remount establishment quartered outside the kingdom in our southern provinces, whence almost all the horses for the Polish cavalry were drawn. For the first time since he went away from home at the age of eighteen to begin his military life by the battle of Friedland, Mr. Nicholas B. breathed the air of the "Border," his native air. Unkind fate was lying in wait for him amongst the scenes of his youth. At the first news of the rising in Warsaw, all the remount establishment, officers, vets., and the very troopers, were put promptly under arrest and hurried off in a body beyond the Dnieper to the nearest town in Russia proper. From there they were dispersed to the distant parts of the Empire. On this occasion poor Mr. Nicholas B. penetrated into Russia much farther than he ever did in the times of Napoleonic invasion, if much less willingly. Astrakhan was his destination. He remained there three years, allowed to live at large in the town, but having to report himself every day at noon to the military commandant, who used to detain him frequently for a pipe and a chat. It is difficult to form a just idea of what a chat with Mr. Nicholas B. could have been like. There must have been much compressed rage under his taciturnity, for the commandant communicated to him the news from the theatre of war, and this news was such as it could be, that is, very bad for the Poles. Mr. Nicholas B. received these communications with outward phlegm, but the Russian showed a warm sympathy for his prisoner. "As a soldier myself I understand your feelings. You, of course, would like to be in the thick of it. By heavens! I am fond of you. If it were not for the terms of the military oath I would let you go on my own responsibility. What difference could it make to us, one more or less of you?"

At other times he wondered with simplicity.

"Tell me, Nicholas Stepanovitch"—(my great-grandfather's name was Stephen and the commandant used the Russian form of polite address)—"tell me why

is it that you Poles are always looking for trouble?
What else could you expect from running up against
Russia?"

He was capable, too, of philosophical reflections.

"Look at your Napoleon now. A great man. There
is no denying it that he was a great man as long as he
was content to thrash those Germans and Austrians
and all those nations. But no! He must go to Russia
looking for trouble, and what's the consequence? Such
as you see me, I have rattled this sabre of mine on the
pavements of Paris."

After his return to Poland Mr. Nicholas B. described
him as a "worthy man but stupid," whenever he could
be induced to speak of the conditions of his exile. Declining the option offered him to enter the Russian
Army, he was retired with only half the pension of his
rank. His nephew (my uncle and guardian) told me
that the first lasting impression on his memory as a
child of four was the glad excitement reigning in his
parents' house on the day when Mr. Nicholas B. arrived
home from his detention in Russia.

Every generation has its memories. The first
memories of Mr. Nicholas B. might have been shaped
by the events of the last partition of Poland, and he
lived long enough to suffer from the last armed rising in
1863, an event which affected the future of all my
generation and has coloured my earliest impressions.

His brother, in whose house he had sheltered for some
seventeen years his misanthropical timidity before the
commonest problems of life, having died in the early
fifties, Mr. Nicholas B. had to screw his courage up to
the sticking-point and come to some decision as to the
future. After a long and agonising hesitation he was
persuaded at last to become the tenant of some fifteen
hundred acres out of the estate of a friend in the

neighbourhood. The terms of the lease were very advantageous, but the retired situation of the village and a plain, comfortable house in good repair were, I fancy, the greatest inducements. He lived there quietly for about ten years, seeing very few people and taking no part in the public life of the province, such as it could be under an arbitrary, bureaucratic tyranny. His character and his patriotism were above suspicion; but the organisers of the rising in their frequent journeys up and down the province scrupulously avoided coming near his house. It was generally felt that the repose of the old man's last years ought not to be disturbed. Even such intimates as my paternal grandfather, a comrade-in-arms during Napoleon's Moscow campaign and later on a fellow-officer in the Polish Army, refrained from visiting his crony as the date of the outbreak approached. My paternal grandfather's two sons and his only daughter were all deeply involved in the revolutionary work; he himself was of that type of Polish squire whose only ideal of patriotic action was to "get into the saddle and drive them out." But even he agreed that "dear Nicholas must not be worried." All this considerate caution on the part of friends, both conspirators and others, did not prevent Mr. Nicholas B. being made to feel the misfortunes of that ill-omened year.

Less than forty-eight hours after the beginning of the rebellion in that part of the country, a squadron of scouting Cossacks passed through the village and invaded the homestead. Most of them remained formed between the house and the stables, while several, dismounting, ransacked the various outbuildings. The officer in command, accompanied by two men, walked up to the front door. All the blinds on that side were down. The officer told the servant who received him that he wanted to see his master. He was answered that the master was away from home, which was perfectly true.

I follow here the tale as told afterwards by the servant to my grand-uncle's friends and relatives, and as I have heard it repeated.

On receiving this answer the Cossack officer, who had been standing in the porch, stepped into the house.

"Where is the master gone, then?"

"Our master went to J——" (the government town some fifty miles off), "the day before yesterday."

"There are only two horses in the stables. Where are the others?"

"Our master always travels with his own horses" (meaning: not by post). "He will be away a week or more. He was pleased to mention to me that he had to attend to some business in the Civil Court."

While the servant was speaking, the officer looked about the hall. There was a door facing him, a door to the right and a door to the left. The officer chose to enter the room on the left and ordered the blinds to be pulled up. It was Mr. Nicholas B.'s study with a couple of tall book-cases, some pictures on the walls, and so on. Besides the big centre table, with books and papers, there was a quite small writing-table with several drawers, standing between the door and the window in a good light; and at this table my grand-uncle usually sat either to read or write.

On pulling up the blind the servant was startled by the discovery that the whole male population of the village was massed in front, trampling down the flower-beds. There were also a few women amongst them. He was glad to observe the village priest (of the Orthodox Church) coming up the drive. The good man in his haste had tucked up his cassock as high as the top of his boots.

The officer had been looking at the backs of the books in the bookcases. Then he perched himself on the edge of the centre table and remarked easily:

"Your master did not take you to town with him then."

"I am the head servant and he leaves me in charge of the house. It's a strong, young chap that travels with our master. If—God forbid—there was some accident on the road he would be of much more use than I."

Glancing through the window he saw the priest arguing vehemently in the thick of the crowd, which seemed subdued by his interference. Three or four men, however, were talking with the Cossacks at the door.

"And you don't think your master has gone to join the rebels, maybe—eh?" asked the officer.

"Our master would be too old for that, surely. He's well over seventy and he's getting feeble too. It's some years now since he's been on horseback and he can't walk much, either, now."

The officer sat there swinging his leg, very quiet and indifferent. By that time the peasants who had been talking with the Cossack troopers at the door had been permitted to get into the hall. One or two more left the crowd and followed them in. They were seven in all and amongst them the blacksmith, an ex-soldier. The servant appealed deferentially to the officer.

"Won't your honour be pleased to tell the people to go back to their homes? What do they want to push themselves into the house like this for? It's not proper for them to behave like this while our master's away, and I am responsible for everything here."

The officer only laughed a little, and after a while inquired:

"Have you any arms in the house?"

"Yes. We have. Some old things."

"Bring them all here, on to this table."

The servant made another attempt to obtain protection.

"Won't your honour tell these chaps . . . ?"

But the officer looked at him in silence in such a way that he gave it up at once and hurried off to call the pantry-boy to help him collect the arms. Meantime the officer walked slowly through all the rooms in the house, examining them attentively but touching nothing. The peasants in the hall fell back and took off their caps when he passed through. He said nothing whatever to them. When he came back to the study all the arms to be found in the house were lying on the table. There was a pair of big flint-lock holster pistols from Napoleonic times, two cavalry swords, one of the French the other of the Polish Army pattern, with a fowling-piece or two.

The officer, opening the window, flung out pistols, swords and guns, one after another, and his troopers ran to pick them up. The peasants in the hall, encouraged by his manner, had stolen after him into the study. He gave not the slightest sign of being conscious of their existence and, his business being apparently concluded, strode out of the house without a word. Directly he left, the peasants in the study put on their caps and began to smile at each other.

The Cossacks rode away, passing through the yards of the home farm straight into the fields. The priest, still arguing with the peasants, moved gradually down the drive and his earnest eloquence was drawing the silent mob after him, away from the house. This justice must be rendered to the parish priests of the Greek Church that, strangers to the country as they were (being all drawn from the interior of Russia), the majority of them used such influence as they had over their flocks in the cause of peace and humanity. True to the spirit of their calling, they tried to soothe the passions of the excited peasantry and opposed rapine and violence, whenever they could, with all their might. And this conduct they pursued against the express wishes of the authorities. Later on some of them were made to suffer for this disobedience by being removed abruptly to the far north or sent away to Siberian parishes.

The servant was anxious to get rid of the few peasants who had got into the house. What sort of conduct was that, he asked them, towards a man who was only a tenant, had been invariably good and considerate to the villagers for years, and only the other day had agreed to give up two meadows for the use of the village herd? He reminded them, too, of Mr. Nicholas B.'s devotion to the sick in the time of cholera. Every word of this was true and so far effective that the fellows began to scratch their heads and look irresolute. The speaker then pointed at the window, exclaiming: "Look! there's all your crowd going away quietly and you silly chaps had better go after them and pray God to forgive you your evil thoughts."

This appeal was an unlucky inspiration. In crowding clumsily to the window to see whether he was speaking the truth, the fellows overturned the little writing-table. As it fell over a chink of loose coin was heard. "There's money in that thing," cried the blacksmith. In a moment the top of the delicate piece of furniture was smashed and there lay exposed in a drawer eighty half-imperials. Gold coin was a rare

sight in Russia even at that time; it put the peasants be-
side themselves. "There must be more of that in the
house and we shall have it," yelled the ex-soldier blacksmith. "This is war time." The others were already
shouting out of the window urging the crowd to come
back and help. The priest, abandoned suddenly at the
gate, flung his arms up and hurried away so as not to
see what was going to happen.

In their search for money that bucolic mob smashed
everything in the house, ripping with knives, splitting
with hatchets, so that, as the servant said, there were no
two pieces of wood holding together left in the whole
house. They broke some very fine mirrors, all the
windows, and every piece of glass and china. They
threw the books and papers out on the lawn and set
fire to the heap for the mere fun of the thing apparently.
Absolutely the only one solitary thing which they left
whole was a small ivory crucifix, which remained hanging on the wall in the wrecked bedroom above a wild
heap of rags, broken mahogany and splintered boards
which had been Mr. Nicholas B.'s bedstead. Detect-
ing the servant in the act of stealing away with a ja-
panned tin box, they tore it from him, and because he
resisted they threw him out of the dining-room window.
The house was on one floor but raised well above the
ground, and the fall was so serious that the man remained lying stunned till the cook and a stable-boy
ventured forth at dusk from their hiding-places and
picked him up. By that time the mob had departed,
carrying off the tin box, which they supposed to be full
of paper money. Some distance from the house in the
middle of a field they broke it open. They found inside documents engrossed on parchment and the two
crosses of the Legion of Honour and For Valour. At
the sight of these objects, which, the blacksmith ex-

plained, were marks of honour given only by the Tsar, they became extremely frightened at what they had done. They threw the whole lot away into a ditch and dispersed hastily.

On learning of this particular loss, Mr. Nicholas B. broke down completely. The mere sacking of his house did not seem to affect him much. While he was still in bed from the shock the two crosses were found and returned to him. It helped somewhat his slow convalescence, but the tin box and the parchments, though searched for in all the ditches around, never turned up again. He could not get over the loss of his Legion of Honour Patent, whose preamble, setting forth his services, he knew by heart to the very letter, and after this blow volunteered sometimes to recite, tears standing in his eyes the while. Its terms haunted him apparently during the last two years of his life to such an extent that he used to repeat them to himself. This is confirmed by the remark made more than once by his old servant to the more intimate friends: "What makes my heart heavy is to hear our master in his room at night walking up and down and praying aloud in the French language."

It must have been somewhat over a year afterwards that I saw Mr. Nicholas B., or, more correctly, that he saw me, for the last time. It was, as I have already said, at the time when my mother had a three-months' leave from exile, which she was spending in the house of her brother, and friends and relations were coming from far and near to do her honour. It is inconceivable that Mr. Nicholas B. should not have been of the number. The little child a few months old he had taken up in his arms on the day of his home-coming after years of war and exile was confessing her faith in national salvation by suffering exile in her turn. I do not know whether he was present on the very day of our departure. I have already admitted that for me he is more especially the man who in his youth had eaten roast dog in the depths of a gloomy forest of snow-loaded pines. My memory cannot place him in any remembered scene. A hooked nose, some sleek white hair, an unrelated evanescent impression of a meagre, slight, rigid figure militarily buttoned up to the throat, is all that now exists on earth of Mr. Nicholas B., only this vague shadow pursued by the memory of his grand-nephew, the last surviving human being, I suppose, of all those he had seen in the course of his taciturn life.

But I remember well the day of our departure back to exile. The elongated, *bizarre*, shabby travelling-carriage with four post-horses, standing before the long front of the house with its eight columns, four on each side of the broad flight of stairs. On the steps, groups of servants, a few relations, one or two friends from the nearest neighbourhood, a perfect silence, on all the faces an air of sober concentration; my grandmother all in black gazing stoically, my uncle giving his arm to my mother down to the carriage in which I had been placed already; at the top of the flight my little cousin in a short skirt of a tartan pattern with a deal of red in it, and like a small princess attended by the women of her own household: the head *gouvernante*, our dear, corpulent Francesca (who had been for thirty years in the service of the B. family), the former nurse, now outdoor attendant, a handsome peasant face wearing a compassionate expression, and the good, ugly Mlle. Durand, the governess, with her black eyebrows meeting over a short thick nose, and a complexion like pale brown paper. Of all the eyes turned towards the carriage, her good-natured eyes only were dropping tears, and it was her sobbing voice alone that broke the silence with an appeal to me: "*N'oublie pas ton français, mon chéri.*" In three months, simply by playing with us, she had taught me not only to speak French but to read it as well. She was indeed an excellent playmate. In the distance, halfway down to the great gates, a light, open trap, harnessed with three horses in Russian fashion, stood drawn up on one side with the police captain of the district sitting in it, the vizor of his flat cap with a red band pulled down over his eyes.

It seems strange that he should have been there to watch our going so carefully. Without wishing to treat with levity the just timidities of Imperialists all the world over, I may allow myself the reflection that a woman, practically condemned by the doctors, and a small boy not quite six years old could not be regarded as seriously dangerous even for the largest of conceivable empires saddled with the most sacred of responsibilities. And this good man, I believe, did not think so either.

I learned afterwards why he was present on that day. I don't remember any outward signs, but it seems that, about a month before, my mother became so unwell that there was a doubt whether she could be made fit to travel in the time. In this uncertainty the Governor-General in Kiev was petitioned to grant her a fortnight's extension of stay in her brother's house. No answer whatever was returned to this prayer, but one day at dusk the police-captain of the district drove up to the house and told my uncle's valet, who ran out to meet him, that he wanted to speak with the master in private, at once. Very much impressed (he thought it was going to be an arrest) the servant, "more dead than alive with fright," as he related afterwards, smuggled him through the big drawing-room which was dark (that room was not lighted every evening), on tiptoe, so as not to attract the attention of the ladies in the house, and led him by way of the orangery to my uncle's private apartments.

The policeman, without any preliminaries, thrust a paper into my uncle's hands.

"There. Pray read this. I have no business to show this paper to you. It is wrong of me. But I can't either eat or sleep with such a job hanging over me."

That police-captain, a native of Great Russia, had been for many years serving in the district.

My uncle unfolded and read the document. It was a service order issued from the Governor-General's secretariat, dealing with the matter of the petition and directing the police-captain to disregard all remonstrances and explanations in regard to that illness either from medical men or others, "and if she has not left her brother's house"—it went on to say—"on the morning of the day specified on her permit, you are to despatch her at once under escort, direct" (underlined) "to the prison-hospital in Kiev, where she will be treated as her case demands."

"For God's sake, Mr. B., see that your sister goes away punctually on that day. Don't give me this work to do with a woman—and with one of your family, too. I simply cannot bear to think of it."

He was absolutely wringing his hands. My uncle looked at him in silence.

"Thank you for this warning. I assure you that even if she were dying she would be carried out to the carriage."

"Yes—indeed—and what difference would it make— travel to Kiev or back to her husband? For she would have to go—death or no death. And mind, Mr. B., I will be here on the day, not that I doubt your promise but because I must. I have got to. Duty. All the same, my trade is not fit for a dog since some of you Poles will persist in rebelling, and all of you have got to suffer for it."

This is the reason why he was there in an open three-horse trap pulled up between the house and the great gates. I regret not being able to give up his name to the scorn of all believers in the rights of conquest, as a reprehensibly sensitive guardian of Imperial greatness. On the other hand, I am in a position to state the name of the Governor-General who signed the order with the marginal note "to be carried out to the letter" in his own handwriting. The gentleman's name was Bezak. A high dignitary, an energetic official, the idol for a time of the Russian Patriotic Press.

Each generation has its memories.

IV

IT MUST not be supposed that in setting forth the memories of this half-hour between the moment my uncle left my room till we met again at dinner, I am losing sight of "Almayer's Folly." Having confessed that my first novel was begun in idleness—a holiday task—I think I have also given the impression that it was a much-delayed book. It was never dismissed from my mind, even when the hope of ever finishing it was very faint. Many things came in its way: daily duties, new impressions, old memories. It was not the outcome of a need—the famous need of self-expression which artists find in their search for motives. The necessity which impelled me was a hidden, obscure necessity, a completely masked and unaccountable phenomenon. Or perhaps some idle and frivolous magician (there must be magicians in London) had cast a spell over me through his parlour window as I explored the maze of streets east and west in solitary leisurely walks without chart and compass. Till I began to write that novel I had written nothing but letters, and not very many of these. I never made a note of a fact, of an impression or of an anecdote in my life. The conception of a planned book was entirely outside my mental range when I sat down to write; the ambition of being an author had never turned up amongst these gracious imaginary existences one creates fondly for oneself at times in the stillness and immobility of a day-dream: yet it stands clear as the sun at noonday that from the moment I had done blackening over the first manuscript page of "Almayer's Folly" (it contained about two hundred words and this proportion of words to a page has remained with me through the fifteen years of my writing life), from the moment I had, in the simplicity of my heart and the amazing ignorance of my mind, written that page the die was cast. Never had Rubicon been more blindly forded, without invocation to the gods, without fear of men.

That morning I got up from my breakfast, pushing the chair back, and rang the bell violently, or perhaps I should say resolutely, or perhaps I should say eagerly, I do not know. But manifestly it must have been a special ring of the bell, a common sound made impressive, like the ringing of a bell for the raising of the curtain upon a new scene. It was an unusual thing for me to do. Generally, I dawdled over my breakfast and I seldom took the trouble to ring the bell for the table to be cleared away; but on that morning for some reason hidden in the general mysteriousness of the event I did not dawdle. And yet I was not in a hurry. I pulled the cord casually, and while the faint tinkling somewhere down in the basement went on, I charged my pipe in the usual way and I looked for the matchbox with glances distraught indeed but exhibiting, I am ready to swear, no signs of a fine frenzy. I was composed enough to perceive after some considerable time the matchbox lying there on the mantelpiece right under my nose. And all this was beautifully and safely usual. Before I had thrown down the match my landlady's daughter appeared with her calm, pale face and an inquisitive look, in the doorway. Of late it was the landlady's daughter who answered my bell. I mention this little fact with pride, because it proves that during the thirty or forty days of my tenancy I had produced a favourable impression. For a fortnight past I had been spared the unattractive sight of the domestic slave. The girls in that Bessborough Gardens house were often changed, but whether short or long, fair or dark, they were always untidy and particularly bedraggled, as if in a sordid version of the fairy tale the ashbin cat had been changed into a maid. I was infinitely sensible of the privilege of being waited on by my landlady's daughter. She was neat if anæmic.

"Will you please clear away all this at once?" I addressed her in convulsive accents, being at the same time engaged in getting my pipe to draw. This, I admit, was an unusual request. Generally on getting up from breakfast I would sit down in the window with a book and let them clear the table when they liked; but if you think that on that morning I was in the least impatient, you are mistaken. I remember that I was perfectly calm. As a matter of fact I was not at all certain that I wanted to write, or that I meant to write, or that I had anything to write about. No, I was not impatient. I lounged between the mantelpiece and the window, not even consciously waiting for the table to be cleared. It was ten to one that before my landlady's daughter was done I would pick up a book and sit down with it all the morning in a spirit of enjoyable indolence. I affirm it with assurance, and I don't even know now what were the books then lying about the room. Whatever they were they were not the works of great masters, where the secret of clear thought and exact expression can be found. Since the age of five I have been a great reader, as is not perhaps wonderful in a child who was never aware of learning to read. At ten years of age I had read much of Victor Hugo and other romantics. I had read in Polish and in French, history, voyages, novels; I knew "Gil Blas" and "Don Quixote" in abridged editions; I had read in early boyhood Polish poets and some French poets, but I cannot say what I read on the evening before I began to write myself. I believe it was a novel, and it is quite possible that it was one of Anthony Trollope's novels. It is very likely. My acquaintance with him was then very recent. He is one of the English novelists whose works I read for the first time in English. With men of European reputation, with Dickens and Walter Scott and Thackeray, it was otherwise. My first introduction to English imaginative literature was "Nicholas Nickleby." It is extraordinary how well Mrs. Nickleby could chatter disconnectedly in Polish and the sinister Ralph rage in that language. As to the Crummles family and the family of the learned Squeers, it seemed as natural to them as their native speech. It was, I have no doubt, an excellent translation. This must have been in the year '70. But I really believe that I am wrong. That book was not my first introduction to English literature. My first acquaintance was (or were) the "Two Gentlemen of Verona," and that in the very MS. of my father's translation. It was during our exile in Russia, and it must have been less than a year after my mother's death, because I remember myself in the black blouse with a white border of my heavy mourning. We were living together, quite alone, in a small house on the outskirts of the town of T———. That afternoon, instead of going out to play in the large yard which we shared with our landlord, I had lingered in the room in which my father generally wrote. What emboldened me to clamber into his chair I am sure I don't know, but a couple of hours afterwards he discovered me kneeling in it with my elbows on the table and my head held in both hands over the MS. of loose pages. I was greatly confused, expecting to get into trouble. He stood in the doorway looking at me with some surprise, but the only thing he said after a moment of silence was:

"Read the page aloud."

Luckily the page lying before me was not over blotted with erasures and corrections, and my father's handwriting was otherwise extremely legible. When I got to the end he nodded and I flew out of doors thinking myself lucky to have escaped reproof for that piece of impulsive audacity. I have tried to discover since the reason of this mildness, and I imagine that all unknown to myself I had earned, in my father's mind, the right to some latitude in my relations with his writing-table. It was only a month before, or perhaps it was only a week before that I had read to him aloud from beginning to end, and to his perfect satisfaction, as he lay on his bed, not being very well at the time, the proofs of his translation of Victor Hugo's "Toilers of the Sea." Such was my title to consideration, I believe, and also my first introduction to the sea in literature. If I do not remember where, how and when I learned to read, I am not likely to forget the process of being trained in the art of reading aloud. My poor father, an admirable reader himself, was the most exacting of masters. I reflect proudly that I must have read that page of "Two Gentlemen of Verona" tolerably well at the age of eight. The next time I met them was in a five shilling one-volume edition of the dramatic works of William Shakespeare, read in Falmouth, at odd moments of the day, to the noisy accompaniment of caulkers' mallets driving oakum into the deck-seams of a ship in dry dock. We had run in, in a sinking condition and with the crew refusing duty after a month of weary battling with the gales of the North Atlantic. Books are an integral part of one's life and my Shakespearean associations are with that first year of our bereavement, the last I spent with my father in exile (he sent me away to Poland to my mother's brother directly he could brace himself up for the separation), and with the year of hard gales, the year in which I came nearest to death at sea, first by water and then by fire.

Those things I remember, but what I was reading the day before my writing life began I have forgotten. I have only a vague notion that it might have been one of Trollope's political novels. And I remember, too, the character of the day. It was an autumn day with an opaline atmosphere, a veiled, semi-opaque, lustrous day, with fiery points and flashes of red sunlight on the roofs and windows opposite, while the trees of the square with all their leaves gone were like tracings of indian ink on a sheet of tissue paper. It was one of those London days that have the charm of mysterious amenity, of fascinating softness. The effect of opaline mist was often repeated at Bessborough Gardens on account of the nearness to the river.

There is no reason why I should remember that effect more on that day than on any other day, except that I stood for a long time looking out of the window after the landlady's daughter was gone with her spoil of cups and saucers. I heard her put the tray down in the passage and finally shut the door; and still I remained smoking with my back to the room. It is very clear that I was in no haste to take the plunge into my writing life, if as plunge this first attempt may be described. My whole being was steeped deep in the indolence of a sailor away from the sea, the scene of never-ending labour and of unceasing duty. For utter surrender to indolence you cannot beat a sailor ashore when that mood is on him, the mood of absolute irresponsibility tasted to the full. It seems to me that I thought of nothing whatever, but this is an impression which is hardly to be believed at this distance of years. What I am certain of is, that I was very far from thinking of writing a story, though it is possible and even likely that I was thinking of the man Almayer.

I had seen him for the first time some four years before from the bridge of a steamer moored to a rickety little wharf forty miles up, more or less, a Bornean river. It was very early morning, and a slight mist, an opaline mist as in Bessborough Gardens only without the fiery flicks on roof and chimney-pot from the rays of the red London sun, promised to turn presently into a woolly fog. Barring a small dug-out canoe on the river, there was nothing moving within sight. I had just come up yawning from my cabin. The serang and the Malay crew were overhauling the cargo chains and trying the winches; their voices sounded subdued on the deck below and their movements were languid. That tropical daybreak was chilly. The Malay quartermaster, coming up to get something from the lockers on the bridge, shivered visibly. The forests above and below and on the opposite bank looked black and dank; wet dripped from the rigging upon the tightly stretched deck awnings, and it was in the middle of a shuddering yawn that I caught sight of Almayer. He was moving across a patch of burnt grass, a blurred, shadowy shape with the blurred bulk of a house behind him, a low house of mats, bamboos and palm-leaves with a high-pitched roof of grass.

He stepped upon the jetty. He was clad simply in flapping pyjamas of cretonne pattern (enormous flowers with yellow petals on a disagreeable blue ground) and a thin cotton singlet with short sleeves. His arms, bare to the elbow, were crossed on his chest. His black hair looked as if it had not been cut for a very long time and a curly wisp of it strayed across his forehead. I had heard of him at Singapore; I had heard of him on board; I had heard of him early in the morning and late at night; I had heard of him at tiffin and at dinner; I had heard of him in a place called Pulo Laut from a half-caste gentleman there, who described himself as the manager of a coal-mine; which sounded civilised and progressive till you heard that the mine could not be worked at present because it was haunted by some particularly atrocious ghosts. I had heard of him in a place called Dongola, in the Island of Celebes, when the Rajah of that little-known sea-port (you can get no anchorage there in less than fifteen fathom, which is extremely inconvenient) came on board in a friendly way with only two attendants, and drank bottle after bottle of soda-water on the after-skylight with my good friend and commander Captain C——. At least I heard his name distinctly pronounced several times in a lot of talk in Malay language. Oh, yes, I heard it quite distinctly—Almayer, Almayer—and saw Captain C—— smile while the fat, dingy Rajah laughed audibly. To hear a Malay Rajah laugh outright is a rare experience, I can assure you. And I overheard more of Almayer's name amongst our deck passengers (mostly wandering traders of good repute) as they sat all over the ship—each man fenced round with bundles and boxes—on mats, on pillows, on quilts, on billets of wood, conversing of Island affairs. Upon my word, I heard the mutter of Almayer's name faintly at midnight, while making my way aft from the bridge to look at the patent taffrail-log tinkling its quarter-miles in the great silence of the sea. I don't mean to say that our passengers dreamed aloud of Almayer, but it is indubitable that two of them at least, who could not sleep apparently and were trying to charm away the trouble of insomnia by a little whispered talk at that ghostly hour were referring in some way or other to Almayer. It was really impossible on board that ship to get away definitely from Almayer; and a very small pony tied up forward and whisking its tail inside the galley, to the great embarrassment of our Chinaman cook, was destined for Almayer. What he wanted with a pony goodness only knows, since I am perfectly certain he could not ride it; but here you have the man, ambitious, aiming at the grandiose, importing a pony, whereas in the whole settlement at which he used to shake daily his impotent fist, there was only one path that was practicable for a pony: a quarter of a mile at most, hedged in by hundreds of square leagues of virgin forest. But who knows? The importation of that Bali pony might have been part of some deep scheme, of some diplomatic plan, of some hopeful intrigue. With Almayer one could never tell. He governed his conduct by considerations removed from the obvious, by incredible assumptions, which rendered his logic impenetrable to any reasonable person. I learned all this later. That morning, seeing the figure in pyjamas moving in the mist, I said to myself: "That's the man."

He came quite close to the ship's side and raised a harassed countenance, round and flat, with that curl of black hair over the forehead and a heavy, pained glance.

"Good morning."

"Good morning."

He looked hard at me: I was a new face, having just replaced the chief mate he was accustomed to see; and I think that this novelty inspired him, as things generally did, with deep-seated mistrust.

"Didn't expect you in till this evening," he remarked suspiciously.

I don't know why he should have been aggrieved, but he seemed to be. I took pains to explain to him that having picked up the beacon at the mouth of the river just before dark and the tide serving, Captain C—— was enabled to cross the bar and there was nothing to prevent him going up the river at night.

"Captain C—— knows this river like his own pocket," I concluded discursively, trying to get on terms.

"Better," said Almayer.

Leaning over the rail of the bridge I looked at Almayer, who looked down at the wharf in aggrieved thought. He shuffled his feet a little; he wore straw slippers with thick soles. The morning fog had thickened considerably. Everything round us dripped: the derricks, the rails, every single rope in the ship—as if a fit of crying had come upon the universe.

Almayer again raised his head and, in the accents of a man accustomed to the buffets of evil fortune, asked hardly audibly: "I suppose you haven't got such a thing as a pony on board?"

I told him almost in a whisper, for he attuned my communications to his minor key, that we had such a thing as a pony, and I hinted, as gently as I could, that he was confoundedly in the way too. I was very anxious to have him landed before I began to handle the cargo. Almayer remained looking up at me for a long while with incredulous and melancholy eyes as though it were not a safe thing to believe my statement. This pathetic mistrust in the favourable issue of any sort of affair touched me deeply, and I added:

"He doesn't seem a bit the worse for the passage. He's a nice pony, too."

Almayer was not to be cheered up; for all answer he cleared his throat and looked down again at his feet. I tried to close with him on another track.

"By Jove!" I said. "Aren't you afraid of catching pneumonia or bronchitis or something, walking about in a singlet in such a wet fog?"

He was not to be propitiated by a show of interest in his health. His answer was a sinister "No fear," as much as to say that even that way of escape from inclement fortune was closed to him.

"I just came down . . ." he mumbled after a while.

"Well, then, now you're here I will land that pony for you at once and you can lead him home. I really don't want him on deck. He's in the way."

Almayer seemed doubtful. I insisted:

"Why, I will just swing him out and land him on the wharf right in front of you. I'd much rather do it before the hatches are off. The little devil may jump down the hold or do some other deadly thing."

"There's a halter?" postulated Almayer.

"Yes, of course there's a halter." And without waiting any more I leaned over the bridge rail.

"Serang, land Tuan Almayer's pony."

The cook hastened to shut the door of the galley and a moment later a great scuffle began on deck. The pony kicked with extreme energy, the kalashes skipped out of the way, the serang issued many orders in a cracked voice. Suddenly the pony leaped upon the fore-hatch. His little hoofs thundered tremendously; he plunged and reared. He had tossed his mane and his forelock into a state of amazing wildness, he dilated his nostrils, bits of foam flecked his broad little chest, his eyes blazed. He was something under eleven hands, he was fierce, terrible, angry, warlike, he said ha! ha! distinctly, he raged and thumped—and sixteen able-bodied kalashes stood round him like disconcerted nurses round a spoilt and passionate child. He whisked his tail incessantly; he arched his pretty neck; he was perfectly delightful; he was charmingly naughty. There was not an atom of vice in that performance; no savage baring of teeth and laying back of ears. On the contrary, he pricked them forward in a comically aggressive manner. He was totally unmoral and lovable; I would have liked to give him bread, sugar, carrots. But life is a stern thing and the sense of duty the only safe guide. So I steeled my heart and from my elevated position on the bridge I ordered the men to fling themselves upon him in a body.

The elderly serang, emitting a strange inarticulate cry, gave the example. He was an excellent petty officer—very competent indeed, and a moderate opium smoker. The rest of them in one great rush smothered that pony. They hung on to his ears, to his mane, to his tail; they lay in piles across his back, seventeen in all. The carpenter, seizing the hook of the cargo-chain, flung himself on the top of them. A very satisfactory petty officer too, but he stuttered. Have you ever heard a light-yellow, lean, sad, earnest Chinaman stutter in pidgin-English? It's very weird indeed. He made the eighteenth. I could not see the pony at all; but from the swaying and heaving of that heap of men I knew that there was something alive inside.

From the wharf Almayer hailed in quavering tones:

"Oh, I say!"

Where he stood he could not see what was going on on deck unless perhaps the tops of the men's heads; he could only hear the scuffle, the mighty thuds as if the ship were being knocked to pieces. I looked over: "What is it?"

"Don't let them break his legs," he entreated me plaintively.

"Oh, nonsense! He's all right now. He can't move."

By that time the cargo-chain had been hooked to the broad canvas belt round the pony's body, the kalashes sprang off simultaneously in all directions, rolling over each other, and the worthy serang, making a dash behind the winch, turned the steam on.

"Steady!" I yelled, in great apprehension of seeing the animal snatched up to the very head of the derrick.

On the wharf Almayer shuffled his straw slippers uneasily. The rattle of the winch stopped, and in a tense, impressive silence that pony began to swing across the deck.

How limp he was! Directly he felt himself in the air he relaxed every muscle in a most wonderful manner. His four hoofs knocked together in a bunch, his head hung down, and his tail remained pendent in a nerveless and absolute immobility. He reminded me vividly of the pathetic little sheep which hangs on the collar of the Order of the Golden Fleece. I had no idea that anything in the shape of a horse could be so limp as that, either living or dead. His wild mane hung down lumpily, a mere mass of inanimate horsehair; his aggressive ears had collapsed, but as he went swaying slowly across the front of the bridge I noticed an astute gleam in his dreamy, half-closed eye. A trustworthy quartermaster, his glance anxious and his mouth on the broad grin, was easing over the derrick watchfully. I superintended, greatly interested.

"So! That will do."

The derrick-head stopped. The kalashes lined the rail. The rope of the halter hung perpendicular and motionless like a bell-pull in front of Almayer. Everything was very still. I suggested amicably that he should catch hold of the rope and mind what he was about. He extended a provokingly casual and superior hand.

"Look out, then! Lower away!"

Almayer gathered in the rope intelligently enough, but when the pony's hoofs touched the wharf he gave way all at once to a most foolish optimism. Without pausing, without thinking, almost without looking, he disengaged the hook suddenly from the sling, and the cargo-chain, after hitting the pony's quarters, swung back against the ship's side with a noisy, rattling slap. I suppose I must have blinked. I know I missed something, because the next thing I saw was Almayer lying flat on his back on the jetty. He was alone.

Astonishment deprived me of speech long enough to give Almayer time to pick himself up in a leisurely and painful manner. The kalashes lining the rail all had their mouths open. The mist flew in the light breeze, and it had come over quite thick enough to hide the shore completely.

"How on earth did you manage to let him get away?" I asked scandalised.

Almayer looked into the smarting palm of his right hand, but did not answer my inquiry.

"Where do you think he will get to?" I cried. "Are there any fences anywhere in this fog? Can he bolt into the forest? What's to be done now?"

Almayer shrugged his shoulders.

"Some of my men are sure to be about. They will get hold of him sooner or later."

"Sooner or later! That's all very fine, but what about my canvas sling?—he's carried it off. I want it now, at once, to land two Celebes cows."

Since Dongola we had on board a pair of the pretty little island cattle in addition to the pony. Tied up on the other side of the fore deck they had been whisking their tails into the other door of the galley. These cows were not for Almayer, however, they were invoiced to Abdullah bin Selim, his enemy. Almayer's disregard of my requirements was complete.

"If I were you I would try to find out where he's gone," I insisted. "Hadn't you better call your men together or something? He will throw himself down and cut his knees. He may even break a leg, you know."

But Almayer, plunged in abstracted thought, did not seem to want that pony any more. Amazed at this sudden indifference, I turned all hands out on shore to hunt for him on my own account, or, at any rate, to hunt for the canvas sling which he had round his body. The whole crew of the steamer, with the exception of firemen and engineers, rushed up the jetty past the thoughtful Almayer and vanished from my sight. The white fog swallowed them up; and again there was a deep silence that seemed to extend for miles up and down the stream. Still taciturn, Almayer started to climb on board, and I went down from the bridge to meet him on the after deck.

"Would you mind telling the captain that I want to see him very particularly?" he asked me in a low tone, letting his eyes stray all over the place.

"Very well. I will go and see."

With the door of his cabin wide open Captain C——, just back from the bath-room, big and broad-chested, was brushing his thick, damp, iron-grey hair with two large brushes.

"Mr. Almayer told me he wanted to see you very particularly, sir."

Saying these words I smiled. I don't know why I smiled except that it seemed absolutely impossible to

imperative conditions of the problem. A refusal would
have appeared perverse and insane. Nobody unless
a surly lunatic would have refused. But if I had not
got to know Almayer pretty well it is almost certain
there would never have been a line of mine in
print.

I accepted then—and I am paying yet the price of
my sanity. The possessor of the only flock of geese on
the East Coast is responsible for the existence of some
fourteen volumes, so far. The number of geese he had
called into being under adverse climatic conditions was
considerably more than fourteen. The tale of volumes
will never overtake the counting of heads, I am safe to
say; but my ambitions point not exactly that way, and
whatever the pangs the toil of writing has cost me I
have always thought kindly of Almayer.

I wonder, had he known anything of it, what his
attitude would have been? This is something not to be
discovered in this world. But if we ever meet in the
Elysian Fields—where I cannot depict him to myself
otherwise than attended in the distance by his flock
of geese (birds sacred to Jupiter)—and he addresses
me in the stillness of that passionless region, neither
light nor darkness, neither sound nor silence, and heaving endlessly with billowy mists from the impalpable
multitudes of the swarming dead, I think I know what
answer to make.

I would say, after listening courteously to the un-
vibrating tone of his measured remonstrances, which
should not disturb, of course, the solemn eternity of
stillness in the least—I would say something like this:

"It is true, Almayer, that in the world below I have
converted your name to my own uses. But that is a
very small larceny. What's in a name, O Shade? If
so much of your old mortal weakness clings to you yet

as to make you feel aggrieved (it was the note of your earthly voice, Almayer), then, I entreat you, seek speech without delay with our sublime fellow-Shade—with him who, in his transient existence as a poet, commented upon the smell of the rose. He will comfort you. You came to me stripped of all prestige by men's queer smiles and the disrespectful chatter of every vagrant trader in the Islands. Your name was the common property of the winds: it, as it were, floated naked over the waters about the Equator. I wrapped round its unhonoured form the royal mantle of the tropics and have essayed to put into the hollow sound the very anguish of paternity—feats which you did not demand from me—but remember that all the toil and all the pain were mine. In your earthly life you haunted me, Almayer. Consider that this was taking a great liberty. Since you were always complaining of being lost to the world, you should remember that if I had not believed enough in your existence to let you haunt my rooms in Bessborough Gardens you would have been much more lost. You affirm that had I been capable of looking at you with a more perfect detachment and a greater simplicity, I might have perceived better the inward marvellousness which, you insist, attended your career upon that tiny pin-point of light, hardly visible, far, far below us, where both our graves lie. No doubt! But reflect, O complaining Shade! that this was not so much my fault as your crowning misfortune. I believed in you in the only way it was possible for me to believe. It was not worthy of your merits? So be it. But you were always an unlucky man, Almayer. Nothing was ever quite worthy of you. What made you so real to me was that you held this lofty theory with some force of conviction and with an admirable consistency."

It is with some such words translated into the proper shadowy expressions that I am prepared to placate Almayer in the Elysian Abode of Shades, since it has come to pass that having parted many years ago, we are never to meet again in this world.

V

IN THE career of the most unliterary of writers, in the sense that literary ambition had never entered the world of his imagination, the coming into existence of the first book is quite an inexplicable event. In my own case I cannot trace it back to any mental or psychological cause which one could point out and hold to. The greatest of my gifts being a consummate capacity for doing nothing, I cannot even point to boredom as a rational stimulus for taking up a pen. The pen at any rate was there, and there is nothing wonderful in that. Everybody keeps a pen (the cold steel of our days) in his rooms in this enlightened age of penny stamps and halfpenny postcards. In fact, this was the epoch when by means of postcard and pen Mr. Gladstone had made the reputation of a novel or two. And I too had a pen rolling about somewhere—the seldom-used, the reluctantly-taken-up pen of a sailor ashore, the pen rugged with the dried ink of abandoned attempts, of answers delayed longer than decency permitted, of letters begun with infinite reluctance and put off suddenly till next day—till next week as likely as not! The neglected, uncared-for pen, flung away at the slightest provocation, and under the stress of dire necessity hunted for without enthusiasm, in a perfunctory, grumpy worry, in the "Where the devil *is* the beastly thing gone to?" ungracious spirit. Where indeed! It might have been reposing behind the sofa for a day or so. My landlady's anæmic daughter (as Ollendorff would have expressed it), though commendably neat, had a lordly, careless manner of approaching her domestic duties. Or it might even be resting delicately poised on its point by the side of the table-leg, and when picked up show a gaping inefficient beak which would have discouraged any man of literary instincts. But not me! "Never mind. This will do."

O days without guile! If anybody had told me then that a devoted household, having a generally exaggerated idea of my talents and importance, would be put into a state of tremor and flurry by the fuss I would make because of a suspicion that somebody had touched my sacrosanct pen of authorship, I would have never deigned as much as the contemptuous smile of unbelief. There are imaginings too unlikely for any kind of notice, too wild for indulgence itself, too absurd for a smile. Perhaps, had that seer of the future been a friend, I should have been secretly saddened. "Alas!" I would have thought, looking at him with an unmoved face, "the poor fellow is going mad."

I would have been, without doubt, saddened; for in this world where the journalists read the signs of the sky, and the wind of heaven itself, blowing where it listeth, does so under the prophetical management of the Meteorological Office, but where the secret of human hearts cannot be captured either by prying or praying, it was infinitely more likely that the sanest of my friends should nurse the germ of incipient madness than that I should turn into a writer of tales.

To survey with wonder the changes of one's own self is a fascinating pursuit for idle hours. The field is so wide, the surprises so varied, the subject so full of unprofitable but curious hints as to the work of unseen forces, that one does not weary easily of it. I am not speaking here of megalomaniacs who rest uneasy under the crown of their unbounded conceit—who really never rest in this world, and when out of it go on fretting and fuming on the straitened circumstances of their last habitation, where all men must lie in obscure equality. Neither am I thinking of those ambitious minds who, always looking forward to some aim of aggrandisement, can spare no time for a detached, impersonal glance upon themselves.

And that's a pity. They are unlucky. These two kinds, together with the much larger band of the totally unimaginative, of those unfortunate beings in whose empty and unseeing gaze (as a great French writer has put it) "the whole universe vanishes into blank nothingness," miss, perhaps, the true task of us men whose day is short on this earth, the abode of conflicting opinions. The ethical view of the universe involves us at last in so many cruel and absurd contradictions, where the last vestiges of faith, hope, charity, and even of reason itself, seem ready to perish, that I have come to suspect that the aim of creation cannot be ethical at all. I would fondly believe that its object is purely spectacular: a spectacle for awe, love, adoration, or hate, if you like, but in this view—and in this view alone—never for despair! Those visions, delicious or poignant, are a moral end in themselves. The rest is our affair—the laughter, the tears, the tenderness, the indignation, the high tranquillity of a steeled heart, the detached curiosity of a subtle mind—that's our affair! And the unwearied self-forgetful attention to every phase of the living universe reflected in our consciousness may be our appointed task on this earth. A task in which fate has perhaps engaged nothing of us except our conscience, gifted with a voice in order to bear true testimony to the visible wonder, the haunting terror, the infinite passion and the illimitable serenity; to the supreme law and the abiding mystery of the sublime spectacle.

Chi lo sà? It may be true. In this view there is room for every religion except for the inverted creed of impiety, the mask and cloak of arid despair; for every joy and every sorrow, for every fair dream, for every charitable hope. The great aim is to remain true to the emotions called out of the deep encircled by the firmament of stars, whose infinite numbers and awful distance may move us to laughter or tears (was it the Walrus or the Carpenter, in the poem, who "wept to see such quantities of sand"?), or, again, to a properly steeled heart, may matter nothing at all.

The casual quotation, which had suggested itself out of a poem full of merit, leads me to remark that in the conception of a purely spectacular universe, where inspiration of every sort has a rational existence, the artist of every kind finds a natural place; and amongst them the poet as the seer *par excellence*. Even the writer of prose, who in his less noble and more toilsome task should be a man with the steeled heart, is worthy of a place, providing he looks on with undimmed eyes and keeps laughter out of his voice, let who will laugh or cry. Yes! Even he, the prose artist of fiction, which after all is but truth often dragged out of a well and clothed in the painted robe of imaged phrases—even he has his place amongst kings, demagogues, priests, charlatans, dukes, giraffes, Cabinet Ministers, Fabians, bricklayers, apostles, ants, scientists, Kaffirs, soldiers, sailors, elephants, lawyers, dandies, microbes and con- stellations of a universe whose amazing spectacle is a moral end in itself.

Here I perceive (speaking without offence) the reader assuming a subtle expression, as if the cat were out of the bag. I take the novelist's freedom to observe the reader's mind formulating the exclamation, "That's it! The fellow talks *pro domo*."

Indeed it was not the intention! When I shouldered the bag I was not aware of the cat inside. But, after all, why not? The fair courtyards of the House of Art are thronged by many humble retainers. And there is no retainer so devoted as he who is allowed to sit on the doorstep. The fellows who have got inside are apt to think too much of themselves. This last remark, I beg to state, is not malicious within the definition of the law of libel. It's fair comment on a matter of public interest. But never mind. *Pro domo.* So be it. For his house *tant que vous voudrez.* And yet in truth I was by no means anxious to justify my existence. The attempt would have been not only needless and absurd but almost inconceivable, in a purely spectacular universe, where no such disagreeable necessity can possibly arise. It is sufficient for me to say (and I am saying it at some length in these pages): *J'ai vécu.* I have existed, obscure amongst the wonders and terrors of my time, as the Abbé Sieyès, the original utterer of the quoted words, had managed to exist through the violences, the crimes, and the enthusiasms of the French Revolution. *J'ai vécu,* as I apprehend most of us manage to exist, missing all along the varied forms of destruction by a hair's-breadth, saving my body, that's clear, and perhaps my soul also, but not without some damage here and there to the fine edge of my conscience, that heirloom of the ages, of the race, of the group, of the family, colourable and plastic, fashioned by the words, the looks, the acts, and even by the silences and abstentions surrounding one's childhood; tinged in a complete scheme of delicate shades and crude colours by the inherited traditions, beliefs, or prejudices— unaccountable, despotic, persuasive, and often, in its texture, romantic.

And often romantic! . . . The matter in hand,

however, is to keep these reminiscences from turning into confessions, a form of literary activity discredited by Jean Jacques Rousseau on account of the extreme thoroughness he brought to the work of justifying his own existence; for that such was his purpose is palpably, even grossly, visible to an unprejudiced eye. But then, you see, the man was not a writer of fiction. He was an artless moralist, as is clearly demonstrated by his anniversaries being celebrated with marked emphasis by the heirs of the French Revolution, which was not a political movement at all, but a great outburst of morality. He had no imagination, as the most casual perusal of "Émile" will prove. He was no novelist, whose first virtue is the exact understanding of the limits traced by the reality of his time to the play of his invention. Inspiration comes from the earth, which has a past, a history, a future, not from the cold and immutable heaven. A writer of imaginative prose (even more than any other sort of artist) stands confessed in his works. His conscience, his deeper sense of things, lawful and unlawful, gives him his attitude before the world. Indeed, everyone who puts pen to paper for the reading of strangers (unless a moralist, who, generally speaking, has no conscience except the one he is at pains to produce for the use of others) can speak of nothing else. It is M. Anatole France, the most eloquent and just of French prose writers, who says that we must recognise at last that, "failing the resolution to hold our peace, we can only talk of ourselves."

This remark, if I remember rightly, was made in the course of a sparring match with the late Ferdinand Brunetière over the principles and rules of literary criticism. As was fitting for a man to whom we owe the memorable saying, "The good critic is he who re-

lates the adventures of his soul amongst masterpieces,"
M. Anatole France maintained that there were no rules
and no principles. And that may be very true. Rules,
principles and standards die and vanish every day.
Perhaps they are all dead and vanished by this time.
These, if ever, are the brave free days of destroyed land-
marks, while the ingenious minds are busy inventing
the forms of the new beacons which, it is consoling to
think, will be set up presently in the old places. But
what is interesting to a writer is the possession of an
inward certitude that literary criticism will never die,
for man (so variously defined) is, before everything
else, a critical animal. And, as long as distinguished
minds are ready to treat it in the spirit of high adventure, literary criticism shall appeal to us with all the
charm and wisdom of a well-told tale of personal experience.

For Englishmen especially, of all the races of the
earth, a task, any task, undertaken in an adventurous
spirit acquires the merit of romance. But the critics
as a rule exhibit but little of an adventurous spirit.
They take risks, of course—one can hardly live without
that. The daily bread is served out to us (however
sparingly) with a pinch of salt. Otherwise one would
get sick of the diet one prays for, and that would be
not only improper, but impious. From impiety of that
or any other kind—save us! An ideal of reserved
manner, adhered to from a sense of proprieties, from
shyness, perhaps, or caution, or simply from weariness,
induces, I suspect, some writers of criticism to conceal
the adventurous side of their calling, and then the
criticism becomes a mere "notice," as it were the
relation of a journey where nothing but the distances
and the geology of a new country should be set down;
the glimpses of strange beasts, the dangers of flood and

field, the hair's-breadth escapes, and the sufferings (oh, the sufferings too! I have no doubt of the sufferings) of the traveller being carefully kept out; no shady spot, no fruitful plant being ever mentioned either; so that the whole performance looks like a mere feat of agility on the part of a trained pen running in a desert. A cruel spectacle—a most deplorable adventure. "Life," in the words of an immortal thinker of, I should say, bucolic origin, but whose perishable name is lost to the worship of posterity—"life is not all beer and skittles." Neither is the writing of novels. It isn't really. *Je vous donne ma parole d'honneur* that it—is—not. Not *all*. I am thus emphatic because some years ago, I remember, the daughter of a general. . .

Sudden revelations of the profane world must have come now and then to hermits in their cells, to the cloistered monks of Middle Ages, to lonely sages, men of science, reformers; the revelations of the world's superficial judgment, shocking to the souls concentrated upon their own bitter labour in the cause of sanctity, or of knowledge, or of temperance, let us say, or of art, if only the art of cracking jokes or playing the flute. And thus this general's daughter came to me—or I should say one of the general's daughters did. There were three of these bachelor ladies, of nicely graduated ages, who held a neighbouring farmhouse in a united and more or less military occupation. The eldest warred against the decay of manners in the village children, and executed frontal attacks upon the village mothers for the conquest of curtseys. It sounds futile, but it was really a war for an idea. The second skirmished and scouted all over the country; and it was that one who pushed a reconnaissance right to my very table—I mean the one who wore stand-up collars. She was really calling upon my wife in the soft spirit of

afternoon friendliness, but with her usual martial
determination. She marched into my room swinging
her stick . . . but no—I mustn't exaggerate. It
is not my speciality. I am not a humoristic writer. In
all soberness, then, all I am certain of is that she had a
stick to swing.

No ditch or wall encompassed my abode. The
window was open; the door too stood open to that best
friend of my work, the warm, still sunshine of the wide
fields. They lay around me infinitely helpful, but truth
to say I had not known for weeks whether the sun shone
upon the earth and whether the stars above still moved
on their appointed courses. I was just then giving up
some days of my allotted span to the last chapters of
the novel "Nostromo," a tale of an imaginary (but
true) seaboard, which is still mentioned now and again,
and indeed kindly, sometimes in connection with the
word "failure" and sometimes in conjunction with the
word "astonishing." I have no opinion on this dis-
crepancy. It's the sort of difference that can never be
settled. All I know, is that, for twenty months,
neglecting the common joys of life that fall to the lot of
the humblest on this earth, I had, like the prophet of
old, "wrestled with the Lord" for my creation, for the
headlands of the coast, for the darkness of the Placid
Gulf, the light on the snows, the clouds on the sky, and
for the breath of life that had to be blown into the
shapes of men and women, of Latin and Saxon, of Jew
and Gentile. These are, perhaps, strong words, but it
is difficult to characterise otherwise the intimacy and
the strain of a creative effort in which mind and will and
conscience are engaged to the full, hour after hour, day
after day, away from the world, and to the exclusion of
all that makes life really lovable and gentle—something
for which a material parallel can only be found in the

everlasting sombre stress of the westward winter passage round Cape Horn. For that too is the wrestling of men with the might of their Creator, in a great isolation from the world, without the amenities and consolations of life, a lonely struggle under a sense of over-matched littleness, for no reward that could be adequate, but for the mere winning of a longitude. Yet a certain longitude, once won, cannot be disputed. The sun and the stars and the shape of your earth are the witnesses of your gain; whereas a handful of pages, no matter how much you have made them your own, are at best but an obscure and questionable spoil. Here they are. "Failure"—"Astonishing": take your choice; or perhaps both, or neither—a mere rustle and flutter of pieces of paper settling down in the night, and undistinguishable, like the snowflakes of a great drift destined to melt away in sunshine.

"How do you do?"

It was the greeting of the general's daughter. I had heard nothing—no rustle, no footsteps. I had felt only a moment before a sort of premonition of evil; I had the sense of an inauspicious presence—just that much warning and no more; and then came the sound of the voice and the jar as of a terrible fall from a great height —a fall, let us say, from the highest of the clouds floating in gentle procession over the fields in the faint westerly air of that July afternoon. I picked myself up quickly, of course; in other words, I jumped up from my chair stunned and dazed, every nerve quivering with the pain of being uprooted out of one world and flung down into another—perfectly civil.

"Oh! How do you do? Won't you sit down?"

That's what I said. This horrible but, I assure you, perfectly true reminiscence tells you more than a whole volume of confessions à la Jean Jacques Rousseau would do. Observe! I didn't howl at her, or start upsetting furniture, or throw myself on the floor and kick, or allow myself to hint in any other way at the appalling magnitude of the disaster. The whole world of Costaguana (the country, you may remember, of my seaboard tale), men, women, headlands, houses, mountains, town, *campo* (there was not a single brick, stone, or grain of sand of its soil I had not placed in position with my own hands); all the history, geography, politics, finance; the wealth of Charles Gould's silver-mine, and the splendour of the magnificent Capataz de Cargadores, whose name, cried out in the night (Dr. Monygham heard it pass over his head—in Linda Viola's voice), dominated even after death the dark gulf containing his conquests of treasure and love—all that had come down crashing about my ears. I felt I could never pick up the pieces— and in that very moment I was saying, "Won't you sit down?"

The sea is strong medicine. Behold what the quarterdeck training even in a merchant ship will do! This episode should give you a new view of the English and Scots seamen (a much-caricatured folk) who had the last say in the formation of my character. One is nothing if not modest, but in this disaster I think I have done some honour to their simple teaching. "Won't you sit down?" Very fair; very fair indeed. She sat down. Her amused glance strayed all over the room. There were pages of MS. on the table and under the table, a batch of typed copy on a chair, single leaves had fluttered away into distant corners; there were there living pages, pages scored and wounded, dead pages that would be burnt at the end of the day—the litter of a cruel battlefield, of a long, long and desperate fray. Long! I suppose I went to bed sometimes, and got up the same number of times. Yes, I suppose I slept, and ate the food put before me, and talked connectedly to my household on suitable occasions. But I had never been aware of the even flow of daily life, made easy and noiseless for me by a silent, watchful, tireless affection. Indeed, it seemed to me that I had been sitting at that table surrounded by the litter of a desperate fray for days and nights on end. It seemed so, because of the intense weariness of which that interruption had made me aware—the awful disenchantment of a mind realising suddenly the futility of an enormous task, joined to a bodily fatigue such as no ordinary amount of fairly heavy physical labour could ever account for. I have carried bags of wheat on my back, bent almost double under a ship's deck-beams, from six in the morning till six in the evening (with an hour and a half off for meals), so I ought to know.

And I love letters. I am jealous of their honour and concerned for the dignity and comeliness of their service. I was, most likely, the only writer that neat lady had ever caught in the exercise of his craft and, it distressed me not to be able to remember when it was that I dressed myself last, and how. No doubt that would be all right in essentials. The fortune of the house included a pair of grey-blue watchful eyes that would see to that. But I felt somehow as grimy as a Costaguana lépero after a day's fighting in the streets, rumpled all over and dishevelled down to my very heels. And I am afraid I blinked stupidly. All this was bad for the honour of letters and the dignity of their service. Seen indistinctly through the dust of my collapsed universe, the good lady glanced about the room with a slightly amused serenity. And she was smiling. What on earth was she smiling at? She remarked casually:

"I am afraid I interrupted you."

"Not at all."

She accepted the denial in perfect good faith. And it was strictly true. Interrupted—indeed! She had robbed me of at least twenty lives, each infinitely more poignant and real than her own, because informed with passion, possessed of convictions, involved in great affairs created out of my own substance for an anxiously meditated end.

She remained silent for a while, then said with a last glance all round at the litter of the fray:

"And you sit like this here writing your—your . . ."

"I—what? Oh, yes! I sit here all day."

"It must be perfectly delightful."

I suppose that, being no longer very young, I might have been on the verge of having a stroke; but she had left her dog in the porch, and my boy's dog, patrolling the field in front, had espied him from afar. He came on straight and swift like a cannon-ball, and the noise of the fight, which burst suddenly upon our ears, was more than enough to scare away a fit of apoplexy. We went out hastily and separated the gallant animals. Afterwards I told the lady where she would find my wife—just round the corner, under the trees. She nodded and went off with her dog, leaving me appalled before the death and devastation she had lightly made— and with the awfully instructive sound of the word "delightful" lingering in my ears.

Nevertheless, later on, I duly escorted her to the field gate. I wanted to be civil, of course (what are twenty lives in a mere novel that one should be rude to a lady on their account?), but mainly, to adopt the good sound Ollendorffian style, because I did not want the dog of the general's daughter to fight again (*encore*) with the faithful dog of my infant son (*mon petit garçon*). —Was I afraid that the dog of the general's daughter would be able to overcome (*vaincre*) the dog of my child?—No, I was not afraid. . . . But away with the Ollendorff method. However appropriate and seemingly unavoidable when I touch upon anything appertaining to the lady, it is most unsuitable to the origin, character and history of the dog; for the dog was the gift to the child from a man for whom words had anything but an Ollendorffian value, a man almost childlike in the impulsive movements of his untutored genius, the most singleminded of verbal impressionists, using his great gifts of straight feeling and right expression with a fine sincerity and a strong, if, perhaps, not fully conscious conviction. His art did not obtain, I fear, all the credit its unsophisticated inspiration deserved. I am alluding to the late Stephen Crane, the author of "The Red Badge of Courage," a work of imagination which found its short moment of celebrity in the last decade of the departed century. Other books followed. Not many. He had not the time. It was an individual and complete talent, which obtained but a grudging, somewhat supercilious recognition from the world at large. For himself one hesitates to regret his early death. Like one of the men in his "Open Boat," one felt that he was of those whom fate seldom allows to make a safe landing after much toil and bitterness at the oar. I confess to an abiding affection for that energetic, slight, fragile, intensely living and transient figure. He liked me even before we met on the strength of a page or two of my writing, and after we had met I am glad to think he liked me still. He used to point out to me with great earnestness, and even with some severity, that "a boy *ought* to have a dog." I suspect that he was shocked at my neglect of parental duties. Ultimately it was he who provided the dog. Shortly afterwards, one day, after playing with the child on the rug for an hour or so with the most intense absorption, he raised his head and declared firmly: "I shall teach your boy to ride." That was not to be. He was not given the time.

But here is the dog—an old dog now. Broad and low on his bandy paws, with a black head on a white body, and a ridiculous black spot at the other end of him, he provokes, when he walks abroad, smiles not altogether unkind. Grotesque and engaging in the whole of his appearance, his usual attitudes are meek, but his temperament discloses itself unexpectedly pugnacious in the presence of his kind. As he lies in the firelight, his head well up, and a fixed, far-away gaze directed at the shadows of the room, he achieves a striking nobility of pose in the calm consciousness of an unstained life. He has brought up one baby, and now, after seeing his first charge off to school, he is bringing up another with the same conscientious devotion but with a more deliberate gravity of manner, the sign of greater wisdom and riper experience, but also of rheumatism, I fear. From the morning bath to the evening ceremonies of the cot you attend, old friend, the little two-legged creature of your adoption, being yourself treated in the exercise of your duties with every possible regard, with infinite consideration, by every person in the house— even as I myself am treated; only you deserve it more. The general's daughter would tell you that it must be "perfectly delightful."

Aha! old dog. She never heard you yelp with acute pain (it's that poor left ear) the while, with incredible self-command, you preserve a rigid immobility for fear of overturning the little two-legged creature. She has never seen your resigned smile when the little two-legged creature, interrogated sternly, "What are you doing to the good dog?" answers with a wide, innocent stare: "Nothing. Only loving him, mamma dear!"

The general's daughter does not know the secret terms of self-imposed tasks, good dog, the pain that may lurk in the very rewards of rigid self-command. But we have lived together many years. We have grown older, too; and though our work is not quite done yet we may indulge now and then in a little introspection before the fire—meditate on the art of bringing up babies and on the perfect delight of writing tales where so many lives come and go at the cost of one which slips imperceptibly away.

VI

In the retrospect of a life which had, besides its preliminary stage of childhood and early youth, two distinct developments, and even two distinct elements, such as earth and water, for its successive scenes, a certain amount of naïveness is unavoidable. I am conscious of it in these pages. This remark is put forward in no apologetic spirit. As years go by and the number of pages grows steadily, the feeling grows upon one too that one can write only for friends. Then why should one put them to the necessity of protesting (as a friend would do) that no apology is necessary, or put, perchance, into their heads the doubt of one's discretion? So much as to the care due to those friends whom a word here, a line there, a fortunate page of just feeling in the right place, some happy simplicity, or even some lucky subtlety, has drawn from the great multitude of fellow-beings even as a fish is drawn from the depths of the sea. Fishing is notoriously (I am talking now of the deep sea) a matter of luck. As to one's enemies, those will take care of themselves.

There is a gentleman, for instance, who, metaphorically speaking, jumps upon me with both feet. This image has no grace, but it is exceedingly apt to the occasion—to the several occasions. I don't know precisely how long he had been indulging in that intermittent exercise, whose seasons are ruled by the custom of the publishing trade. Somebody pointed him out (in printed shape, of course) to my attention some time ago, and straightway I experienced a sort of reluctant affection for that robust man. He leaves not a shred of my substance untrodden: for the writer's substance is his writing; the rest of him is but a vain shadow, cherished or hated on uncritical grounds. Not a shred! Yet the sentiment owned to is not a freak of affectation or perversity. It has a deeper, and, I venture to think, a more estimable origin than the caprice of emotional lawlessness. It is, indeed, lawful in so much that it is given (reluctantly) for a consideration, for several considerations. There is that robustness, for instance, so often the sign of good moral balance. That's a consideration. It is not, indeed, pleasant to be stamped upon, but the very thoroughness of the operation, implying not only a careful reading, but some real insight into work whose qualities and defects, whatever they may be, are not so much on the surface, is something to be thankful for in view of the fact that it may happen to one's work to be condemned without being read at all. This is the most fatuous adventure that can well happen to a writer venturing his soul amongst criticisms. It can do one no harm, of course, but it is disagreeable. It is disagreeable in the same way as discovering a three-card-trick man amongst a decent lot of folk in a third-class compartment. The open impudence of the whole transaction, appealing insidiously to the folly and credulity of mankind, the brazen, shameless patter, proclaiming the fraud openly while insisting on the fairness of the game, give one a feeling of sickening disgust. The honest violence of a plain man playing a fair game fairly—even if he means to knock you over—may appear shocking, but it remains within the pale of decency. Damaging as it may be, it is in no sense offensive. One may well feel some regard for honesty, even if practised upon one's own vile body. But it is very obvious that an enemy of that sort will not be stayed by explanations or placated by apologies. Were I to advance the plea of youth in excuse of the naïveness to be found in these pages, he would be likely to say "Bosh!" in a column and a half of fierce print. Yet a writer is no older than his first published book, and, notwithstanding the vain appearances of decay which attend us in this transitory life, I stand here with the wreath of only fifteen short summers on my brow.

With the remark, then, that at such tender age, some naïveness of feeling and expression is excusable, I proceed to admit that, upon the whole, my previous state of existence was not a good equipment for a literary life. Perhaps I should not have used the word literary. That word presupposes an intimacy of acquaintance with letters, a turn of mind and a manner of feeling to which I dare lay no claim. I only love letters; but the love of letters does not make a literary man, any more than the love of the sea makes a seaman. And it is very possible too, that I love the letters in the same way a literary man may love the sea he looks at from the shore—a scene of great endeavour and of great achievements changing the face of the world, the great open way to all sorts of undiscovered countries. No, perhaps I had better say that the life at sea—and I don't mean a mere taste of it, but a good broad span of years, something that really counts as real service—is not, upon the whole, a good equipment for a writing life. God forbid, though, that I should be thought of as denying my masters of the quarter-deck. I am not capable of that sort of apostasy. I have confessed my attitude of piety towards their shades in three or four tales, and if any man on earth more than another needs to be true to himself as he hopes to be saved, it is certainly the writer of fiction.

What I meant to say, simply, is that the quarter-deck training does not prepare one sufficiently for the reception of literary criticism. Only that, and no more. But this defect is not without gravity. If it be permissible to twist, invert, adapt (and spoil) M. Anatole France's definition of a good critic, then let us say that the good author is he who contemplates without marked joy or excessive sorrow the adventures of his soul amongst criticisms. Far be from me the intention to mislead an attentive public into the belief that there is no criticism at sea. That would be dishonest, and even impolite. Everything can be found at sea, according to the spirit of your quest—strife, peace, romance, naturalism of the most pronounced kind, ideals, boredom, disgust, inspiration—and every conceivable opportunity, including the opportunity to make a fool of yourself—exactly as in the pursuit of literature. But the quarter-deck criticism is somewhat different from literary criticism. This much they have in common, that before the one and the other the answering back, as a general rule, does not pay.

Yes, you find criticism at sea, and even appreciation— I tell you everything is to be found on salt water—criticism generally impromptu, and always *viva voce*, which is the outward, obvious difference from the literary operation of that kind, with consequent freshness and vigour which may be lacking in the printed word. With appreciation, which comes at the end, when the critic and the criticised are about to part, it is otherwise. The sea appreciation of one's humble talents has the permanency of the written word, seldom the charm of variety, is formal in its phrasing. There the literary master has the superiority, though he, too, can in effect but say —and often says it in the very phrase—"I can highly recommend." Only usually he uses the word "We," there being some occult virtue in the first person plural, which makes it specially fit for critical and royal declarations. I have a small handful of these sea appreciations, signed by various masters, yellowing slowly in my writing-table's left-hand drawer, rustling under my reverent touch, like a handful of dry leaves plucked for a tender memento from the tree of knowledge. Strange! It seems that it is for these few bits of paper, headed by the names of a few ships and signed by the names of a few Scots and English shipmasters, that I have faced the astonished indignations, the mockeries and the reproaches of a sort hard to bear for a boy of fifteen; that I have been charged with the want of patriotism, the want of sense, and the want of heart too; that I went through agonies of self-conflict and shed secret tears not a few, and had the beauties of the Furca Pass spoiled for me, and have been called an "incorrigible Don Quixote," in allusion to the book-born madness of the knight. For that spoil! They rustle, those bits of paper—some dozen of them in all. In that faint, ghostly sound there live the memories of twenty years, the voices of rough men now no more, the strong voice of the everlasting winds, and the whisper of a mysterious spell, the murmur of the great sea, which must have somehow reached my inland cradle and entered my unconscious ear, like that formula of Mohammedan faith the Mussulman father whispers into the ear of his new-born infant, making him one of the faithful almost with his first breath. I do not know whether I have been a good seaman, but I know I have been a very faithful one. And after all there is that handful of "characters" from various ships to prove that all these years have not been altogether a dream. There they are, brief, and monotonous in tone, but as suggestive bits of writing to me as any inspired page to

be found in literature. But then, you see, I have been
called romantic. Well, that can't be helped. But
stay. I seem to remember that I have been called a
realist also. And as that charge too can be made out,
let us try to live up to it, at whatever cost, for a change.
With this end in view, I will confide to you coyly, and
only because there is no one about to see my blushes by
the light of the midnight lamp, that these suggestive bits
of quarter-deck appreciation one and all contain the
words "strictly sober."

Did I overhear a civil murmur, "That's very gratifying to be sure"? Well, yes, it is gratifying—thank you.
It is at least as gratifying to be certified sober as to be
certified romantic, though such certificates would not
qualify one for the secretaryship of a temperance association or for the post of official troubadour to some
lordly democratic institution such as the London
County Council, for instance. The above prosaic reflection is put down here only in order to prove the
general sobriety of my judgment in mundane affairs.
I make a point of it because a couple of years ago, a
certain short story of mine being published in a French
translation, a Parisian critic—I am almost certain it
was M. Gustave Kahn, in the *Gil-Blas*—giving me a
short notice, summed up his rapid impression of the
writer's quality in the words *un puissant rêveur*. So
be it! Who would cavil at the words of a friendly
reader? Yet perhaps not such an unconditional
dreamer as all that. I will make bold to say that
neither at sea nor ashore have I ever lost the sense of
responsibility. There is more than one sort of in-
toxication. Even before the most seductive reveries I
have remained mindful of that sobriety of interior life,
that asceticism of sentiment, in which alone the naked
form of truth, such as one conceives it, such as one feels

it, can be rendered without shame. It is but a maudlin
and indecent verity that comes out through the strength
of wine. I have tried to be a sober worker all my life—
all my two lives. I did so from taste, no doubt, having
an instinctive horror of losing my sense of full self-
possession, but also from artistic conviction. Yet
there are so many pitfalls on each side of the true path
that, having gone some way, and feeling a little battered
and weary, as a middle-aged traveller will from the
mere daily difficulties of the march, I ask myself
whether I have kept always, always faithful to that
sobriety wherein there is power, and truth, and peace.

As to my sea-sobriety, that is quite properly certified
under the sign-manual of several trustworthy shipmasters of some standing in their time. I seem to hear
your polite murmur that "Surely this might have been
taken for granted." Well, no. It might not have
been. That august academical body of the Marine
Department of the Board of Trade takes nothing for
granted in the granting of its learned degrees. By its
regulations issued under the first Merchant Shipping
Act, the very word SOBER must be written, or a whole
sackful, a ton, a mountain of the most enthusiastic
appreciation will avail you nothing. The door of the
examination rooms shall remain closed to your tears
and entreaties. The most fanatical advocate of temperance could not be more pitilessly fierce in his rectitude
than the Marine Department of the Board of Trade.
As I have been face to face at various times with all the
examiners of the Port of London, in my generation,
there can be no doubt as to the force and the continuity
of my abstemiousness. Three of them were examiners
in seamanship, and it was my fate to be delivered into
the hands of each of them at proper intervals of sea
service. The first of all, tall, spare, with a perfectly

white head and moustache, a quiet, kindly manner, and an air of benign intelligence, must, I am forced to conclude, have been unfavourably impressed by something in my appearance. His old thin hands loosely clasped resting on his crossed legs, he began by an elementary question in a mild voice, and went on, went on . . . It lasted for hours, for hours. Had I been a strange microbe with potentialities of deadly mischief to the Merchant Service I could not have been submitted to a more microscopic examination. Greatly reassured by his apparent benevolence, I had been at first very alert in my answers. But at length the feeling of my brain getting addled crept upon me. And still the passionless process went on, with a sense of untold ages having been spent already on mere preliminaries. Then I got frightened. I was not frightened of being plucked; that eventuality did not even present itself to my mind. It was something much more serious, and weird. "This ancient person," I said to myself, terrified, "is so near his grave that he must have lost all notion of time. He is considering this examination in terms of eternity. It is all very well for him. His race is run. But I may find myself coming out of this room into the world of men a stranger, friendless, forgotten by my very landlady, even were I able after this endless experience to remember the way to my hired home." This statement is not so much of a verbal exaggeration as may be supposed. Some very queer thoughts passed through my head while I was considering my answers; thoughts which had nothing to do with seamanship, nor yet with anything reasonable known to this earth. I verily believe that at times I was lightheaded in a sort of languid way. At last there fell a silence, and that, too, seemed to last for ages, while, bending over his desk, the examiner wrote out my pass-slip slowly with a noiseless pen.

He extended the scrap of paper to me without a word, inclined his white head gravely to my parting bow . . .

When I got out of the room I felt limply flat, like a squeezed lemon, and the doorkeeper in his glass cage, where I stopped to get my hat and tip him a shilling, said:

"Well! I thought you were never coming out."

"How long have I been in there?" I asked faintly.

He pulled out his watch.

"He kept you, sir, just under three hours. I don't think this ever happened with any of the gentlemen before."

It was only when I got out of the building that I began to walk on air. And the human animal being averse from change and timid before the unknown, I said to myself that I would not mind really being examined by the same man on a future occasion. But when the time of ordeal came round again the doorkeeper let me into another room, with the now familiar paraphernalia of models of ships and tackle, a board for signals on the wall, a big long table covered with official forms, and having an unrigged mast fixed to the edge. The solitary tenant was unknown to me by sight, though not by reputation, which was simply execrable. Short and sturdy as far as I could judge, clad in an old, brown, morning suit, he sat leaning on his elbow, his hand shading his eyes, and half averted from the chair I was to occupy on the other side of the table. He was motionless, mysterious, remote, enigmatical, with something mournful too in the pose, like that statue of Giuliano (I think) de Medici shading his face on the tomb by Michael Angelo, though, of course, he was far, far from being beautiful. He began by trying to make me talk nonsense. But I had been warned of that fiendish trait, and contradicted him with great

assurance. After a while he left off. So far, good.
But his immobility, the thick elbow on the table, the
abrupt, unhappy voice, the shaded and averted face
grew more and more impressive. He kept inscrutably
silent for a moment, and then, placing me in a ship of a
certain size at sea, under certain conditions of weather,
season, locality, etc., etc.—all very clear and precise—
ordered me to execute a certain manœuvre. Before I
was half through with it he did some material damage
to the ship. Directly I had grappled with the difficulty
he caused another to present itself, and when that too
was met he stuck another ship before me, creating a very
dangerous situation. I felt slightly outraged by this
ingenuity in piling up trouble upon a man.

"I wouldn't have got into that mess," I suggested
mildly. "I could have seen that ship before."

He never stirred the least bit.

"No, you couldn't. The weather's thick."

"Oh! I didn't know," I apologised blankly. I suppose that after all I managed to stave off the smash with
sufficient approach to verisimilitude, and the ghastly
business went on. You must understand that the
scheme of the test he was applying to me was, I gathered,
a homeward passage—the sort of passage I would not
wish to my bitterest enemy. That imaginary ship
seemed to labour under a most comprehensive curse.
It's no use enlarging on these never-ending misfortunes;
suffice it to say that long before the end I would have
welcomed with gratitude an opportunity to exchange
into the *Flying Dutchman*. Finally he shoved me into
the North Sea (I suppose) and provided me with a lee-
shore with outlying sandbanks—the Dutch coast pre-
sumably. Distance, eight miles. The evidence of such
implacable animosity deprived me of speech for quite
half a minute.

"Well," he said—for our pace had been very smart indeed till then.

"I will have to think a little, sir."

"Doesn't look as if there were much time to think," he muttered sardonically from under his hand.

"No, sir," I said with some warmth. "Not on board a ship I could see. But so many accidents have happened that I really can't remember what there's left for me to work with."

Still half averted, and with his eyes concealed, he made unexpectedly a grunting remark.

"You've done very well."

"Have I the two anchors at the bow, sir?" I asked. "Yes."

I prepared myself then, as a last hope for the ship, to let them both go in the most effectual manner, when his infernal system of testing resourcefulness came into play again.

"But there's only one cable. You've lost the other."

It was exasperating.

"Then I would back them, if I could, and tail the heaviest hawser on board on the end of the chain before letting go, and if she parted from that, which is quite likely, I would just do nothing. She would have to go."

"Nothing more to do, eh?"

"No, sir. I could do no more."

He gave a bitter half-laugh.

"You could always say your prayers."

He got up, stretched himself, and yawned slightly. It was a sallow, strong, unamiable face. He put me in a surly, bored fashion through the usual questions as to lights and signals, and I escaped from the room thankfully—passed! Forty minutes! And again I walked on air along Tower Hill, where so many good men had

lost their heads, because, I suppose, they were not re-
sourceful enough to save them. And in my heart of
hearts I had no objection to meeting that examiner
once more when the third and last ordeal became due in
another year or so. I even hoped I should. I knew the
worst of him now, and forty minutes is not an unreasonable time. Yes, I distinctly hoped . . .

But not a bit of it. When I presented myself to be
examined for Master the examiner who received me
was short, plump, with a round, soft face in grey, fluffy
whiskers, and fresh, loquacious lips.

He commenced operations with an easy-going "Let's
see. H'm. Suppose you tell me all you know of
charter-parties." He kept it up in that style all
through, wandering off in the shape of comment into
bits out of his own life, then pulling himself up short
and returning to the business in hand. It was very
interesting. "What's your idea of a jury-rudder now?"
he queried suddenly, at the end of an instructive anecdote bearing upon a point of stowage.

I warned him that I had no experience of a lost rudder
at sea, and gave him two classical examples of make-
shifts out of a text-book. In exchange he described to
me a jury-rudder he had invented himself years before,
when in command of a 3000-ton steamer. It was, I
declare, the cleverest contrivance imaginable. "May
be of use to you some day," he concluded. "You
will go into steam presently. Everybody goes into
steam."

There he was wrong. I never went into steam—not
really. If I only live long enough I shall become a
bizarre relic of a dead barbarism, a sort of monstrous
antiquity, the only seaman of the dark ages who had
never gone into steam—not really.

Before the examination was over he imparted to me

a few interesting details of the transport service in the time of the Crimean War.

"The use of wire rigging became general about that time too," he observed. "I was a very young master then. That was before you were born."

"Yes, sir. I am of the year 1857."

"The Mutiny year," he commented, as if to himself adding in a louder tone that his ship happened then to be in the Gulf of Bengal, employed under a Government charter.

Clearly the transport service had been the making of this examiner, who so unexpectedly had given me an insight into his existence, awakening in me the sense of the continuity of that sea-life into which I had stepped from outside; giving a touch of human intimacy to the machinery of official relations. I felt adopted. His experience was for me, too, as though he had been an ancestor.

Writing my long name (it has twelve letters) with laborious care on the slip of blue paper, he remarked:

"You are of Polish extraction."

"Born there, sir."

He laid down the pen and leaned back to look at me as it were for the first time.

"Not many of your nationality in our service, I should think. I never remember meeting one either before or after I left the sea. Don't remember ever hearing of one. An inland people, aren't you?"

I said yes—very much so. We were remote from the sea not only by situation, but also from a complete absence of indirect association, not being a commercial nation at all, but purely agricultural. He made then the quaint reflection that it was "a long way for me to come out to begin a sea-life"; as if sea-life were not precisely a life in which one goes a long way from home.

I told him, smiling, that no doubt I could have found a ship much nearer my native place, but I had thought to myself that if I was to be a seaman then I would be a British seaman and no other. It was a matter of deliberate choice.

He nodded slightly at that; and as he kept on looking at me interrogatively, I enlarged a little, confessing that I had spent a little time on the way in the Mediterranean and in the West Indies. I did not want to present myself to the British Merchant Service in an altogether green state. It was no use telling him that my mysterious vocation was so strong that my very wild oats had to be sown at sea. It was the exact truth, but he would not have understood the somewhat exceptional psychology of my sea-going, I fear.

"I suppose you've never come across one of your countrymen at sea. Have you now?"

I admitted I never had. The examiner had given himself up to the spirit of gossiping idleness. For myself, I was in no haste to leave that room. Not in the least. The era of examinations was over. I would never again see that friendly man who was a professional ancestor, a sort of grandfather in the craft. Moreover, I had to wait till he dismissed me, and of that there was no sign. As he remained silent, looking at me, I added:

"But I have heard of one, some years ago. He seems to have been a boy serving his time on board a Liverpool ship, if I am not mistaken."

"What was his name?"

I told him.

"How did you say that?" he asked, puckering up his eyes at the uncouth sound.

I repeated the name very distinctly.

"How do you spell it?"

I told him. He moved his head at the impracticable nature of that name, and observed:

"It's quite as long as your own—isn't it?"

There was no hurry. I had passed for Master, and I had all the rest of my life before me to make the best of it. That seemed a long time. I went leisurely through a small mental calculation, and said:

"Not quite. Shorter by two letters, sir."

"Is it?" The examiner pushed the signed blue slip across the table to me, and rose from his chair. Somehow this seemed a very abrupt ending of our relations, and I felt almost sorry to part from that excellent man, who was master of a ship before the whisper of the sea had reached my cradle. He offered me his hand and wished me well. He even made a few steps towards the door with me, and ended with good-natured advice.

"I don't know what may be your plans but you ought to go into steam. When a man has got his master's certificate it's the proper time. If I were you I would go into steam."

I thanked him, and shut the door behind me definitely on the era of examinations. But that time I did not walk on air, as on the first two occasions. I walked across the Hill of many beheadings with measured steps. It was a fact, I said to myself, that I was now a British master mariner beyond a doubt. It was not that I had an exaggerated sense of that very modest achievement, with which, however, luck, opportunity, or any extraneous influence could have had nothing to do. That fact, satisfactory and obscure in itself, had for me a certain ideal significance. It was an answer to certain outspoken scepticism, and even to some not very kind aspersions. I had vindicated myself from what had been cried upon as a stupid obstinacy or a fantastic caprice. I don't mean to say that a whole country

had been convulsed by my desire to go to sea. But
for a boy between fifteen and sixteen, sensitive enough,
in all conscience, the commotion of his little world had
seemed a very considerable thing indeed. So considerable that, absurdly enough, the echoes of it linger to this
day. I catch myself in hours of solitude and retrospect
meeting arguments and charges made thirty-five years
ago by voices now for ever still; finding things to say
that an assailed boy could not have found, simply because of the mysteriousness of his impulses to himself.
I understood no more than the people who called upon
me to explain myself. There was no precedent. I
verily believe mine was the only case of a boy of my
nationality and antecedents taking a, so to speak,
standing jump out of his racial surroundings and
associations. For you must understand that there was
no idea of any sort of "career" in my call. Of Russia
or Germany there could be no question. The nationality, the antecedents, made it impossible. The feeling
against the Austrian service was not so strong, and I
dare say there would have been no difficulty in finding
my way into the Naval School at Pola. It would have
meant six months' extra grinding at German, perhaps,
but I was not past the age of admission, and in other
respects I was well qualified. This expedient to palliate
my folly was thought of—but not by me. I must admit that in that respect my negative was accepted at
once. That order of feeling was comprehensible
enough to the most inimical of my critics. I was not
called upon to offer explanations; the truth is that what
I had in view was not a naval career, but the sea.
There seemed no way open to it but through France. I
had the language at any rate, and of all the countries
in Europe it is with France that Poland has most connection. There were some facilities for having me a

little looked after, at first. Letters were being written, answers were being received, arrangements were being made for my departure for Marseilles, where an excellent fellow called Solary, got at in a roundabout fashion through various French channels, had promised good-naturedly to put *le jeune homme* in the way of getting a decent ship for his first start if he really wanted a taste of *ce métier de chien.*

I watched all these preparations gratefully, and kept my own counsel. But what I told the last of my examiners was perfectly true. Already the determined resolve, that "if a seaman, then an English seaman," was formulated in my head though, of course, in the Polish language. I did not know six words of English, and I was astute enough to understand that it was much better to say nothing of my purpose. As it was I was already looked upon as partly insane, at least by the more distant acquaintances. The principal thing was to get away. I put my trust in the good-natured Solary's very civil letter to my uncle, though I was shocked a little by the phrase about the *métier de chien.*

This Solary (Baptistin), when I beheld him in the flesh, turned out a quite young man, very good-looking, with a fine black, short beard, a fresh complexion, and soft, merry black eyes. He was as jovial and good-natured as any boy could desire. I was still asleep in my room in a modest hotel near the quays of the old port, after the fatigues of the journey *via* Vienna, Zurich, Lyons, when he burst in, flinging the shutters open to the sun of Provence and chiding me boisterously for lying abed. How pleasantly he startled me by his noisy objurgations to be up and off instantly for a "three years' campaign in the South Seas." O magic words! "*Une campagne de trois ans dans les mers du sud*"—that is the French for a three years' deep-water voyage.

He gave me a delightful waking, and his friendliness was unwearied; but I fear he did not enter upon the quest for a ship for me in a very solemn spirit. He had been at sea himself, but had left off at the age of twenty-five, finding he could earn his living on shore in a much more agreeable manner. He was related to an incredible number of Marseilles well-to-do families of a certain class. One of his uncles was a ship-broker of good standing, with a large connection amongst English ships; other relatives of his dealt in ships' stores, owned sail-lofts, sold chains and anchors, were master-stevedores, caulkers, shipwrights. His grandfather (I think) was a dignitary of a kind, the Syndic of the Pilots. I made acquaintances amongst these people, but mainly amongst the pilots. The very first whole day I ever spent on salt water was by invitation, in a big half-decked pilot-boat, cruising under close reefs on the lookout, in misty, blowing weather, for the sails of ships and the smoke of steamers rising out there, beyond the slim and tall Planier lighthouse cutting the line of the wind-swept horizon with a white perpendicular stroke. They were hospitable souls, these sturdy Provençal seamen. Under the general designation of *le petit ami de Baptistin* I was made the guest of the Corporation of Pilots, and had the freedom of their boats night or day. And many a day and a night too did I spend cruising with these rough, kindly men, under whose auspices my intimacy with the sea began. Many a time "the little friend of Baptistin" had the hooded cloak of the Mediterranean sailor thrown over him by their honest hands while dodging at night under the lee of Château d'If on the watch for the lights of ships. Their sea-tanned faces, whiskered or shaved, lean or full, with the

intent wrinkled sea-eyes of the pilot-breed, and here
and there a thin gold loop at the lobe of a hairy ear,
bent over my sea-infancy. The first operation of seamanship I had an opportunity of observing was the
boarding of ships at sea, at all times, in all states of the
weather. They gave it to me to the full. And I have
been invited to sit in more than one tall, dark house of
the old town at their hospitable board, had the *bouilla-
baisse* ladled out into a thick plate by their high-voiced,
broad-browed wives, talked to their daughters—thick-
set girls, with pure profiles, glorious masses of black
hair arranged with complicated art, dark eyes, and
dazzlingly white teeth.

I had also other acquaintances of quite a different
sort. One of them, Madame Delestang, an imperious,
handsome lady in a statuesque style, would carry me
off now and then on the front seat of her carriage to the
Prado, at the hour of fashionable airing. She belonged
to one of the old aristocratic families in the south. In
her haughty weariness she used to make me think of
Lady Dedlock in Dickens' "Bleak House," a work of
the master for which I have such an admiration, or
rather such an intense and unreasoning affection, dating
from the days of my childhood, that its very weaknesses are more precious to me than the strength of
other men's work. I have read it innumerable times,
both in Polish and in English; I have read it only the
other day, and, by a not very surprising inversion, the
Lady Dedlock of the book reminded me strongly of the
belle Madame Delestang.

Her husband (as I sat facing them both), with his
thin bony nose, and a perfectly bloodless, narrow
physiognomy clamped together as it were by short
formal side-whiskers, had nothing of Sir Leicester
Dedlock's "grand air" and courtly solemnity. He

belonged to the *haute bourgeoisie* only, and was a banker, with whom a modest credit had been opened for my needs. He was such an ardent—no, such a frozen-up, mummified Royalist that he used in current conversation turns of speech contemporary, I should say, with the good Henri Quatre; and when talking of money matters reckoned not in francs, like the common, godless herd of post-Revolutionary Frenchmen, but in obsolete and forgotten *écus—écus* of all money units in the world!—as though Louis Quatorze were still promenading in royal splendour the gardens of Versailles, and Monsieur de Colbert busy with the direction of maritime affairs. You must admit that in a banker of the nineteenth century it was a quaint idiosyncrasy. Luckily in the counting-house (it occupied part of the ground floor of the Delestang town residence, in a silent, shady street) the accounts were kept in modern money so that I never had any difficulty in making my wants known to the grave, low-voiced, decorous, Legitimist (I suppose) clerks, sitting in the perpetual gloom of heavily-barred windows behind the sombre, ancient counters, beneath lofty ceilings with heavily-moulded cornices. I always felt on going out as though I had been in the temple of some very dignified but completely temporal religion. And it was generally on these occasions that under the great carriage gateway Lady Ded—I mean Madame Delestang, catching sight of my raised hat, would beckon me with an amiable imperiousness to the side of the carriage, and suggest with an air of amused nonchalance, "*Venez donc faire un tour avec nous*," to which the husband would add an encouraging "*C'est ça. Allons, montez, jeune homme.*" He questioned me sometimes, significantly but with perfect tact and delicacy, as to the way I employed my time, and never failed to express the hope that I wrote regularly to my "honoured uncle." I made no secret of the way I employed my time, and I rather fancy that my artless tales of the pilots and so on entertained Madame Delestang, so far as that ineffable woman could be entertained by the prattle of a youngster very full of his new experience amongst strange men and strange sensations. She expressed no opinions, and talked to me very little; yet her portrait hangs in the gallery of my intimate memories, fixed there by a short and fleeting episode. One day, after putting me down at the corner of a street, she offered me her hand, and detained me by a slight pressure, for a moment. While the husband sat motionless and looking straight before him, she leaned forward in the carriage to say, with just a shade of warning in her leisurely tone: "*Il faut, cependant, faire attention à ne pas gâter sa vie.*" I had never seen her face so close to mine before. She made my heart beat, and caused me to remain thoughtful for a whole evening. Certainly one must, after all, take care not to spoil one's life. But she did not know—nobody could know—how impossible that danger seemed to me.

VII

CAN the transports of first love be calmed, checked, turned to a cold suspicion of the future by a grave quotation from a work on Political Economy? I ask—Is it conceivable? Is it possible? Would it be right? With my feet on the very shores of the sea and about to embrace my blue-eyed dream, what could a good-natured warning as to spoiling one's life mean to my youthful passion? It was the most unexpected and the last, too, of the many warnings I had received. It sounded to me very *bizarre*—and, uttered as it was in the very presence of my enchantress, like the voice of folly, the voice of ignorance. But I was not so callous or so stupid as not to recognise there also the voice of kindness. And then the vagueness of the warning—because what can be the meaning of the phrase: to spoil one's life?—arrested one's attention by its air of wise profundity. At any rate, as I have said before, the words of *la belle Madame Delestang* made me thoughtful for a whole evening. I tried to understand and tried in vain, not having any notion of life as an enterprise that could be mismanaged. But I left off being thoughtful shortly before midnight, at which hour, haunted by no ghosts of the past and by no visions of the future, I walked down the quay of the *Vieux Port* to join the pilot-boat of my friends. I knew where she would be waiting for her crew, in the little bit of a canal behind the Fort at the entrance of the harbour. The deserted quays looked very white and dry in the moonlight and as if frost-bound in the sharp air of that December night.

A prowler or two slunk by noiselessly; a custom-house guard, soldier-like, a sword by his side, paced close under the bowsprits of the long row of ships moored bows on opposite the long, slightly curved, continuous flat wall of the tall houses that seemed to be one immense abandoned building with innumerable windows shuttered closely. Only here and there a small dingy *café* for sailors cast a yellow gleam on the bluish sheen of the flagstone. Passing by, one heard a deep murmur of voices inside—nothing more. How quiet everything was at the end of the quays on the last night on which I went out for a service cruise as a guest of the Marseilles pilots! Not a footstep, except my own, not a sigh, not a whispering echo of the usual revelry going on in the narrow, unspeakable lanes of the Old Town reached my ear—and suddenly, with a terrific jingling rattle of iron and glass, the omnibus of the Jolliette on its last journey swung round the corner of the dead wall which faces across the paved road the characteristic angular mass of the Fort St. Jean. Three horses trotted abreast with the clatter of hoofs on the granite setts, and the yellow, uproarious machine jolted violently behind them, fantastic, lighted up, perfectly empty and with the driver apparently asleep on his swaying perch above that amazing racket. I flattened myself against the wall and gasped. It was a stunning experience. Then after staggering on a few paces in the shadow of the Fort casting a darkness more intense than that of a clouded night upon the canal, I saw the tiny light of a lantern standing on the quay, and became aware of muffled figures making towards it from various directions—Pilots of the Third Company hastening to embark. Too sleepy to be talkative, they step on board in silence. But a few low grunts and an enormous yawn are heard. Somebody even ejaculates:

"*Ah! Coquin de sort!*" and sighs wearily at his hard fate.

The *patron* of the Third Company (there were five companies of pilots at that time, I believe) is the brother-in-law of my friend Solary (Baptistin), a broad-shouldered, deep-chested man of forty, with a keen, frank glance which always seeks your eyes. He greets me by a low, hearty "*Hé, l'ami. Comment va?*" With his clipped moustache and massive open face, energetic and at the same time placid in expression, he is a fine specimen of the southerner of the calm type. For there is such a type in which the volatile southern passion is transmuted into solid force. He is fair, but no one could mistake him for a man of the north even by the dim gleam of the lantern standing on the quay. He is worth a dozen of your ordinary Normans or Bretons, but then, in the whole immense sweep of the Mediterranean shores, you could not find half a dozen men of his stamp.

Standing by the tiller, he pulls out his watch from under a thick jacket and bends his head over it in the light cast into the boat. Time's up. His pleasant voice commands in a quiet undertone, "*Larguez.*" A suddenly projected arm snatches the lantern off the quay—and, warped along by a line at first, then with the regular tug of four heavy sweeps in the bow, the big half-decked boat full of men glides out of the black, breathless shadow of the Fort. The open water of the *avant-port* glitters under the moon as if sown over with millions of sequins, and the long white breakwater shines like a thick bar of solid silver. With a quick rattle of blocks and one single silky swish, the sail is filled by a little breeze keen enough to have come straight down from the frozen moon, and the boat, after the clatter of the hauled-in sweeps, seems to stand at rest, surrounded by a mysterious whispering so faint and unearthly that it may be the rustling of the brilliant, overpowering moonrays breaking like a rain-shower upon the hard, smooth, shadowless sea.

I may well remember that last night spent with the pilots of the Third Company. I have known the spell of moonlight since, on various seas and coasts —coasts of forests, of rocks, of sand dunes—but no magic so perfect in its revelation of unsuspected character, as though one were allowed to look upon the mystic nature of material things. For hours I suppose no word was spoken in that boat. The pilots seated in two rows facing each other dozed with their arms folded and their chins resting upon their breasts. They displayed a great variety of caps: cloth, wool, leather, ear-flaps, tassels, with a picturesque round *béret* or two pulled down over the brows; and one grandfather, with a shaved, bony face and a great beak of a nose, had a cloak with a hood which made him look in our midst like a cowled monk being carried off goodness knows where by that silent company of seamen—quiet enough to be dead.

My fingers itched for the tiller, and in due course my friend, the *patron*, surrendered it to me in the same spirit in which the family coachman lets a boy hold the reins on an easy bit of road. There was a great solitude around us; the islets ahead, Monte Cristo and the Château d'If in full light, seemed to float towards us— so steady, so imperceptible was the progress of our boat. "Keep her in the furrow of the moon," the *patron* directed me in a quiet murmur, sitting down ponderously in the stern-sheets and reaching for his pipe.

The pilot station in weather like this was only a mile or two to the westward of the islets; and presently, as we approached the spot, the boat we were going to

relieve swam into our view suddenly, on her way home,
cutting black and sinister into the wake of the moon
under a sable wing, while to them our sail must have
been a vision of white and dazzling radiance. Without
altering the course a hair's-breadth, we slipped by
each other within an oar's-length. A drawling sardonic
hail came out of her. Instantly, as if by magic, our
dozing pilots got on their feet in a body. An incredible
babel of bantering shouts burst out, a jocular, passionate, voluble chatter, which lasted till the boats were
stern to stern, theirs all bright now and with a shining
sail to our eye, we turned all black to their vision, and
drawing away from them under a sable wing. That
extraordinary uproar died away almost as suddenly
as it had begun; first one had enough of it and sat down,
then another, then three or four together, and when all
had left off with mutters and growling half-laughs the
sound of hearty chuckling became audible, persistent,
unnoticed. The cowled grandfather was very much
entertained somewhere within his hood.

He had not joined in the shouting of jokes, neither
had he moved the least bit. He had remained quietly
in his place against the foot of the mast. I had been
given to understand long before that he had the rating of
a second-class able seaman (*matelot léger*) in the fleet
which sailed from Toulon for the conquest of Algeria in
the year of grace 1830. And, indeed, I had seen and
examined one of the buttons of his old brown patched
coat, the only brass button of the miscellaneous lot,
flat and thin, with the words *Equipages de ligne* engraved
on it. That sort of button, I believe, went out with the
last of the French Bourbons. "I preserved it from the
time of my Navy Service," he explained, nodding
rapidly his frail, vulture-like head. It was not very
likely that he had picked up that relic in the street. He

looked certainly old enough to have fought at Trafalgar
—or at any rate to have played his little part there as a
powder-monkey. Shortly after we had been introduced
he had informed me in a Franco-Provençal jargon,
mumbling tremulously with his toothless jaws, that
when he was a "shaver no higher than that" he had
seen the Emperor Napoleon returning from Elba. It
was at night, he narrated vaguely, without animation,
at a spot between Fréjus and Antibes in the open
country. A big fire had been lit at the side of the
cross-roads. The population from several villages had
collected there, old and young—down to the very
children in arms because the women had refused to
stay at home. Tall soldiers, wearing high, hairy caps,
stood in a circle facing the people silently, and their
stern eyes and big moustaches were enough to make
everybody keep at a distance. He, "being an im-
pudent little shaver," wriggled out of the crowd, creep-
ing on his hands and knees as near as he dared to the
grenadiers' legs, and peeping through discovered standing perfectly still in the light of the fire "a little fat
fellow in a three-cornered hat, buttoned up in a long
straight coat, with a big pale face, inclined on one
shoulder, looking something like a priest. His hands
were clasped behind his back . . . It appears that
this was the Emperor," the Ancient commented with
a faint sigh. He was staring from the ground with all
his might, when "my poor father," who had been
searching for his boy frantically everywhere, pounced
upon him and hauled him away by the ear.

The tale seems an authentic recollection. He related it to me many times, using the very same words.
The grandfather honoured me by a special and somewhat embarrassing predilection. Extremes touch. He
was the oldest member by a long way in that Company,

spired talent of Mr. Jacobs for poking endless fun at poor, innocent sailors in a prose which, however extravagant in its felicitous invention, is always artistically adjusted to observed truth, was not yet. Perhaps Mr. Jacobs himself was not yet. I fancy that, at most, if he had made his nurse laugh it was about all he had achieved at that early date.

Therefore, I repeat, other disabilities apart, I could not have been prepared for the sight of that husky old porpoise. The object of his concise address was to call my attention to a rope which he incontinently flung down for me to catch. I caught it, though it was not really necessary, the ship having no way on her by that time. Then everything went on very swiftly. The dinghy came with a slight bump against the steamer's side, the pilot, grabbing the rope ladder, had scrambled half-way up before I knew that our task of boarding was done; the harsh, muffled clanging of the engine-room telegraph struck my ear through the iron plate; my companion in the dinghy was urging me to "shove off— push hard"; and when I bore against the smooth flank of the first English ship I ever touched in my life, I felt it already throbbing under my open palm.

Her head swung a little to the west, pointing towards the miniature lighthouse of the Jolliette breakwater, far away there, hardly distinguishable against the land. The dinghy danced a squashy, splashy jig in the wash of the wake and turning in my seat I followed the *James Westoll* with my eyes. Before she had gone in a quarter of a mile she hoisted her flag as the harbour regulations prescribe for arriving and departing ships. I saw it suddenly flicker and stream out on the flagstaff. The Red Ensign! In the pellucid, colourless atmosphere bathing the drab and grey masses of that southern land, the livid islets, the sea of pale glassy blue under the pale glassy sky of that cold sunrise, it was, as far as the eye could reach, the only spot of ardent colour—flamelike, intense, and presently as minute as the tiny red spark the concentrated reflection of a great fire kindles in the clear heart of a globe of crystal. The Red Ensign—the symbolic, protecting warm bit of bunting flung wide upon the seas, and destined for so many years to be the only roof over my head.

THE END